Legal Aspects of Infectious Diseases

Benjamin Tanner, Ph.D.

Lawyers & Judges Publishing Company, Inc.
Tucson, Arizona

This publication is designed to provide accurate and authoritative information in regard to the subject matter covered. It is sold with the understanding that the publisher is not engaged in rendering legal, accounting, or other professional service. If legal advice or other expert assistance is required, the services of a competent professional should be sought.

—From a *Declaration of Principles* jointly adopted by a committee of the American Bar Association and a committee of publishers and associations.

The publisher, editors and authors must disclaim any liability, in whole or in part, arising from the information in this volume. The reader is urged to verify the reference material prior to any detrimental reliance thereupon. Since this material deals with legal, medical and engineering information, the reader is urged to consult with an appropriate licensed professional prior to taking any action that might involve any interpretation or application of information within the realm of a licensed professional practice.

Lawyers & Judges Publishing Company, Inc.
P.O. Box 30040 • Tucson, AZ 85751-0040
(800) 209-7109 • FAX (800) 330-8795
e-mail: sales@lawyersandjudges.com

Library of Congress Cataloging-in-Publication Data

Tanner, Benjamin, 1979-
Legal aspects of infectious diseases / Benjamin Tanner.
p. cm.
Includes bibliographical references.
ISBN-13: 978-1-930056-92-3 (pbk.)
1. Communicable diseases. 2. Medical jurisprudence. I. Title.
RC111.T36 2006
614'.1--dc22

2006016998

ISBN 1-930056-92-3
Printed in the United States of America
10 9 8 7 6 5 4 3 2 1

online
www.lawyersandjudges.com

I dedicate this book to my loving wife, father, and mother.

Thank you for everything.

— Benjamin Tanner

Contents

Acknowledgments

I wish to express my appreciation to Dr. Charles Gerba for taking the time to review this work and Dr. Gordon Vrdoljak for providing the electron micrograph that appears on the cover. I would also like to thank Krista Arendsen and Steve Weintraub of Lawyers and Judges Publishing for all of their insight and hard work throughout the creation of this book.

— Benjamin Tanner

Preface

This book is designed to help legal professionals accurately and self-assuredly litigate infectious disease claims by providing practical information about microorganisms and disease transmission. It spans three professional disciplines and myriad specific areas of study and can serve as an informative guide to the science of infectious diseases or a handy resource during litigation. The first part of this book discusses infectious disease litigation generally, including the role of the expert witness and the types of claims that are likely to arise. Next, the reader is introduced to microorganisms and microbiology in an accurate, yet understandable, way. Infectious diseases are described, grouped by mode of disease transmission, such that lawyers, judges, epidemiologists, microbiologists, and physicians can locate salient information without trouble. Finally, the book addresses malevolent use of microorganisms and discusses how risks of infection can be estimated accurately and communicated appropriately to the public. By reading this book, you will gain a well-rounded understanding of infectious diseases and disease transmission that will help to prepare for success during infectious disease litigation.

Chapter 1

Infectious Disease Litigation

Synopsis

1.1 Chapter Preview

Infectious diseases are a common source of litigation in the United States. Cases arise in several ways, involve different types of disease-causing microorganisms, and have various outcomes. Plaintiffs generally must show that their disease was caused by a specific exposure to microorganisms and that exposure was negligent in order to collect damages. Expert witnesses are a key part of infectious disease litigation and include physicians, microbiologists, and epidemiologists. Lawyers who are interested in infectious disease litigation can enhance their probability of success by understanding the science of infectious diseases and by choosing the right expert witness to complement a sound legal strategy.

1.2 Introduction

Infectious diseases and associated litigation arise from a litany of sources, including medical malpractice, improper sanitation, inadequate disinfection of drinking water, contamination of recreational water, carelessness during food production and handling, substandard building construction and maintenance, and risky occupations. Infections transmitted in hospitals are a major concern. In fact, one in ten people admitted to a hospital will leave with a hospital-acquired infection (Filetoth 2003). Foodborne diseases are also important. Recent litigation stemming from illnesses and deaths caused by *E. coli* O157:H7 bacteria in undercooked meat at a large fast-food chain was eventually settled out of court for up to 15 million dollars per case (Marler 2005). Waterborne infectious diseases are relevant because they have the potential to affect thousands of people and can be prevented by adequate water treatment. In 1993, the parasite *Cryptosporidium parvum* made 400,000 people sick and killed around 100 when it was spread through contaminated public drinking water in Milwaukee, Wisconsin. Recreational water can also spark litigation. Hundreds of people have contracted Legionnaire's Disease from exposure to aerosols generated by contaminated spas. In addition, poorly constructed or maintained buildings can expose people to raw sewage and mold, which often results in litigation. Lastly, certain occupations increase risks of infection and can cause litigation, such as employment in a wastewater treatment plant, hospital or farm (Keefe 2004, Short 1993, and others).

Infectious disease litigation usually centers on acute, or short term, symptoms of an infection, but chronic symptoms can also be important. Acute symptoms are experienced during the initial phase of an infection by a large percentage of those infected. For example, sore throat with white patches, weakness, and fever are all acute symptoms of strep throat. Chronic symptoms of infection, called sequelae, come about after the acute phase of the disease has passed and usually affect a smaller percentage of those infected. For example, rheumatic fever is a chronic symptom of strep throat. Rheumatic fever develops when the immune system attacks proteins on the heart after the strep throat has cleared, mistakenly believing that the heart proteins are part of the bacterium that caused the strep throat. Other examples of infectious disease sequelae include certain types of arthritis, heart disease, diabetes, fatigue, and cancer, which have been linked in some way to specific infections by microorganisms. Acute symptoms of disease are relatively easy to explain or present; everyone understands how food poisoning or viral hepatitis causes pain and suffering. However, sequelae are challenging because some are controversial and poorly understood; most people don't understand how a sexually transmitted disease can lead to cervical cancer or how a *Staphylococcus* infection can cause heart disease.

A great deal of infectious disease litigation revolves around the ability of a claimant to show that a particular microorganism from a particular source actually caused the disease. All things considered, people are exposed to disease-causing microorganisms many times a day, thus a good scientific argument must be made to show that an infectious disease was spread by a particular exposure to microorganisms. This is usually done in one of two ways. First, specimens from an infected person and from a suspected source of microorganisms can be analyzed in a laboratory for a "match." If the same strain of microorganism is found in the infected person as is found in the suspected source, then it is highly likely that the suspected source of the disease was actually responsible for the infection. Sometimes samples are not available for scientific analysis, such as when a hamburger presumed to have contained *E. coli* is thrown away or a catheter suspected to have been contaminated with *Pseudomonas aeruginosa* is sterilized. When samples cannot be analyzed, claimants must build a case that their disease was caused by a particular source of exposure to a microorganism on the basis of expert witness testimony. Expert witnesses can include epidemiologists, doctors, and microbiologists. Expert witness testimony carries a great deal of weight during infectious disease litigation. Experts will estimate the probability of the disease-causing microorganism having been in the suspected location at the time of infection. In these cases, a lawyer's knowledge of infectious diseases is crucial for establishing an expert's authority or impeaching witnesses with controversial or speculative theories.

Judges and lawyers may have to sift through "junk science" or contradictory studies during infectious disease litigation. Like scientists in other fields, microbiologists frequently differ by the scientific theories they accept and reject, and by the studies they believe to be credible. In theory, the scientific value of an infectious disease study depends only on the experimental method used and its reproducibility. Unfortunately, funding sources, experimental errors, and manipulation of data (statistical or otherwise) can affect conclusions.

Some interesting precedents have been set with respect to infectious diseases. For example, courts have held that people with certain types of infections are entitled to special treatment under the law. Specifically the

United States Supreme Court held that individuals suffering from infections with HIV, whether showing the symptoms of infection or not, are protected under the Americans with Disabilities Act, *See Bragdon v. Abbott 118 S.Ct. 2196 (U.S. 1998)*. Courts have also held that infected people are legally accountable for spreading infectious diseases maliciously or negligently.

1.3 Claims

Claims arising from infections usually fall under the umbrella of "toxic-tort" litigation, and come about when a serious disease is transmitted to one or many people negligently. Infectious disease claims can raise a number of questions for legal professionals, including the following: What really happened? How many people were affected? How much damage was done? Was exposure to the microorganism abnormally risky? Can this be proven or demonstrated? (Figure 1.1)

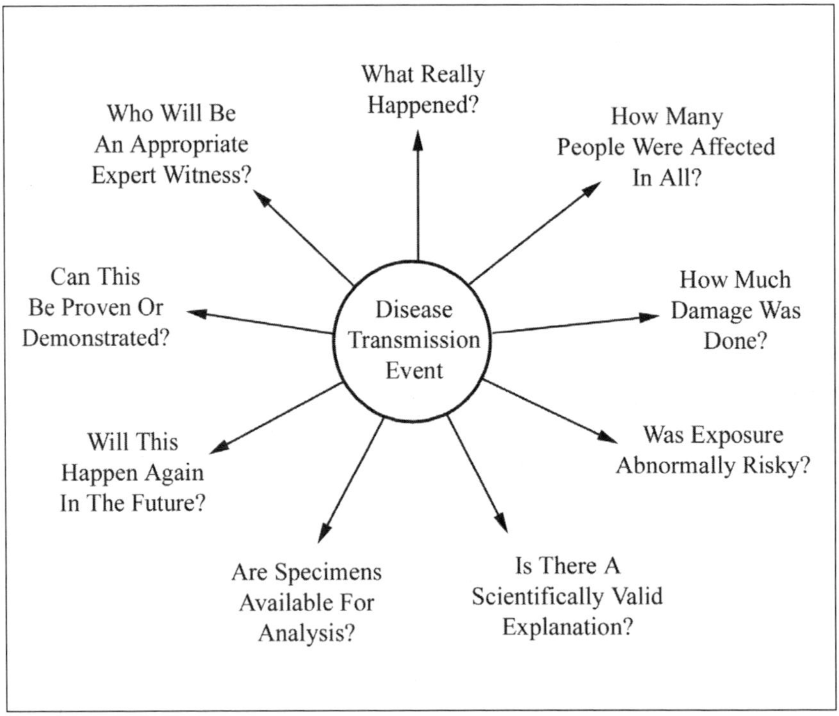

Figure 1.1 *Questions associated with disease transmission.*

In most cases, claimants seek compensation for pain and suffering caused by an infectious disease, believing that they would not have been exposed to the disease agent under normal circumstances. Various legal theories can be applied to infectious disease claims, including negligence, breach of contract, battery, violation of implied warranty, trespass, and misrepresentation. To successfully bring a toxic tort claim, a plaintiff must prove three things. First, they must show that they were exposed to a contaminant in some way. Second, they must show that they were exposed to a sufficient level of the contaminant to cause harm. Lastly, they must show that the contaminant actually caused their injury. This places a great burden on plaintiffs' attorneys (Rubin 2003). To show that a plaintiff was exposed to a contaminant, plaintiffs' attorneys must demonstrate that the microorganisms of interest were actually present in the suspected source of the disease. For example, if the suspected source of the disease was water, then exposure to the contaminant could be demonstrated through a positive microbiological culture or a good scientific argument that the microorganism was present based on other factors. Showing exposure to sufficient levels of a microorganism to cause harm is the second step successfully bringing a toxic-tort claim. This is linked to the notion that some "infectious dose" of a microorganism is needed to initiate an infection. In practice, the number of microorganisms needed to cause infection depends on a variety of factors, including the nature and infectivity of the microbe and the immune status of the host. Mathematical dose-response models are the best way to estimate the number of microorganisms needed to cause an infection. These models are usually developed through volunteer studies, in which people are paid to ingest various doses of disease-causing microorganisms but can also come from retrospective analysis of infectious disease outbreaks. The last part of bringing a toxic-tort claim is demonstrating that the microorganism in question actually caused the specified injury. A positive clinical specimen can show this concretely. If clinical specimens were not taken or are not available, physicians can assess the likelihood that the disease was caused by a particular microorganism based on symptoms observed or described at the time of infection.

In most cases, the plaintiff must also prove that the defendant was negligent or at fault in order to collect damages (Marler 2005). Specifically, the plaintiff must show that the defendant breached a duty of care and caused an injury for which compensation should be provided (Rubin 2003). Consider the following three examples. If the owner of a hamburger shop knew that a day's supply of hamburger had been left on a countertop for a few hours while the refrigerator was being cleaned, yet served the hamburger to customers anyway, he or she would be at risk of transmitting a disease negligently. If a drinking water treatment plant operator knew that the facility's chlorination system was functioning erratically, yet did not take corrective action, he or she would be at risk of transmitting a disease negligently. If a nurse at a hospital left a catheter in a patient for a couple of days longer than typically because he or she was pressed for time, that person would be at risk of transmitting a disease negligently. All of the people mentioned in these examples have a duty of care and knowledge that their negligence could result in disease transmission. In addition, all fell below the general and accepted professional standards of conduct in the performance of their jobs.

1.4 The Expert Witness

Experts can aid lawyers throughout infectious disease litigation. They can perform diagnostic microbiology or epidemiological studies to identify or confirm the source of a disease. Experts also can provide criticism of past tests and identify weaknesses in scientific arguments. Some also can relay firsthand experience with infectious diseases to lawyers, judges, and jurors to strengthen cases. Experts also can help to assess the extent of damages caused by an infectious disease.

Physicians, microbiologists, and epidemiologists are the three types of expert witnesses usually involved in infectious disease litigation. Physicians play a key role because they have a high degree of public respect, formal microbiology training, and an experience-based perspective of infectious diseases. In some cases, the physician serving as an expert witness will have diagnosed the infection in question. Physicians base their diagnosis of the causative agent of an infection on laboratory analysis of clinical samples or disease symptoms of the patient. Although physicians usually have a broad knowledge base, their depth of understanding with respect to a particular infectious disease or transmission route may be limited relative to that of an expert microbiologist. There are three types of expert microbiologists who can support infectious disease litigation. The first is the academic expert microbiologist. They usually have a Doctor of Philosophy Degree (Ph.D.) and perform focused research on specific microorganisms or problems, usually for a university. They are especially useful for providing the theoretical grounds for scientific arguments used in the courtroom. The second is the diagnostic microbiologist. They are trained to isolate and identify various microorganisms and usually work for clinical diagnostic laboratories. They are an excellent resource for lawyers who are attempting to establish or critique a link between microorganisms isolated from the environment and patients. Epidemiologists are the third type of expert witness commonly involved in infectious disease litigation. They collect and analyze statistical information about outbreaks, under the assumption that disease does not occur randomly but rather in discernible patterns that show the underlying cause of the disease (Friis 1999). Epidemiology is a remarkably interdisciplinary field, strongly connected to statistics, public health, microbiology, and toxicology. Epidemiologists are most useful in situations when the argument that a disease was caused by a particular exposure is based on correlation of events. It is important to choose a well-qualified expert witness because not all experts have expertise in all areas, and the study of infectious diseases encompasses a broad range of disciplines.

A lawyer's choice of expert witness has great bearing on the direction and success of infectious disease litigation. Lawyers may want to first consider whether an expert with a high degree of technical depth or one with a broad understanding of the field would better serve their case. Experts with extensive technical knowledge of a subject tend to benefit cases where the scientific plausibility of disease transmission is at question, whereas experts with a broader knowledge base tend to benefit cases centering on the probability of disease transmission. A good expert witnesses will be able to convey complex science to laypeople accurately, have good scientific reputation and ability, and have a focus of study that complements the issue at hand. The appearance of bias or poor scientific judgment in an expert witness should be avoided at all costs. Most cases will involve at least two expert witnesses with opposing views about the nature or scope of the infectious disease in question. This can be challenging. The best way for lawyers and judges to handle such circumstances is to have a broad, accurate knowledge base that enables them to detect bogus theories and to choose experts who complement their overarching legal strategy.

1.5 Chapter Summary

Infectious disease litigation occurs as a result of medical malpractice, improper sanitation, inadequate disinfection of drinking water, contaminated recreational water, careless food production and handling, poor building construction or maintenance, and risky occupations. In order to collect damages, a plaintiff must usually show that an infectious disease was transmitted negligently. To prove causation, claimants must show that they were exposed to the contaminant at a sufficient level to cause disease and that the contaminant actually caused their disease. Expert witnesses play a key role in infectious disease litigation and include physicians, microbiologists, and epidemiologists.

Chapter 2

Overview of Microbes and Infection

Synopsis

2.1 Chapter Preview

This chapter provides lawyers and judges with an overview of microorganisms and infectious diseases and the impact they have on individuals and society. A brief history of microbiology is given and the various routes of disease transmission are introduced. The omnipresence of microbial life is emphasized and disease-causing microorganisms are distinguished from those that are generally harmless. This chapter introduces the four main types of microorganisms that impact our health and the ways in which our immune systems interact with them. In addition, this chapter describes some of the subtle and indirect consequences of infections. By reading this chapter, lawyers and judges will gain a broad economical, historical, and scientific perspective of infectious diseases that is fundamental to more specific discussions later in this book.

2.2 Introduction

Our bodies and the objects around us are teeming with invisible forms of life, known scientifically as microorganisms. Microorganisms can be found living in nearly every part of Earth, including Antarctica and the atmosphere. More than one hundred thousand species have been identified so far and thousands more surely remain undiscovered. Some microorganisms are so small that a million of them could fit side-by-side on the period at the end of this sentence. Some are so devastating that they end lives every few seconds. Some are so useful that people could not live without them. Microbiology is the large, diverse and rapidly evolving discipline that studies microorganisms.

Some microorganisms cause infectious diseases and have great impact on human life and civilization. Scientists have only known that microorganisms cause infectious diseases for the last two centuries, but people have taken measures to control the spread of infectious diseases for millennia. Ancient civilizations built infrastructure and developed customs, laws, and medicine to help control the spread of infectious diseases. In modern times, infectious diseases are controlled in much the same way, through public sanitation systems, medicine, and hygienic practices like handwashing. Infectious diseases impact individuals by reducing productivity and causing pain, bodily damage, or death. Infectious diseases impact societies in an equally dramatic fashion. The spread of smallpox virus, for example, eradicated entire civilizations (Diamond 1999).

Humans have made great progress in combating infectious diseases, but challenges still remain. Water disinfection, vaccines, and antibiotics have drastically reduced the impact of infectious diseases. Recent outbreaks of Sudden Acute Respiratory Syndrome (SARS) virus appear to demonstrate that novel and highly infectious microorganisms can be quickly identified and controlled using modern science. But globalization, the spread of Human Immunodeficiency Virus (HIV) and the emergence of antibiotic resistance among bacteria make it clear that infectious diseases will remain a challenge to scientists and legal professionals for the foreseeable future.

2.3 A Brief History of Microbiology

Before people understood that microorganisms caused infectious diseases, they adopted behaviors that appeared to offer protection from infectious diseases. Early on, people learned that avoiding the places where ill people lived offered protection from disease. Seneca (c. 4 B.C. – 65 A.D.) even wrote, "Disease is not of the body but of the place." For example, lepers were shunned to control the spread of leprosy and people would flee to the countryside in Europe during the great plague epidemics. Eventually, careful observations led to new ways to protect people from infectious diseases. For example, people observed that milkmaids who contracted cowpox were frequently immune to smallpox. Since cowpox infection is mild relative to smallpox, people deliberately exposed themselves to cowpox to protect themselves from smallpox. In another example, Catholic nuns observed that boiling their garments in vinegar afforded them some protection from bubonic plague in Florence, Italy in the seventeenth century. They didn't understand why the vinegar protected them, but it worked nonetheless. In retrospect, the vinegar probably repelled the bacteria-harboring fleas that transmitted the plague, thereby protecting the nuns. By the time microorganisms were revealed to be the cause of infectious diseases in the nineteenth century, people had already developed many ways to protect themselves from infectious diseases.

In the same way that astronomy boomed after the invention of the telescope, microbiology blossomed after the invention of the microscope. An Englishman named Robert Hooke (1635–1703) made many observations using a microscope and was the first to observe microscopic fungi. Around the same time, a cloth merchant from Holland named Anton van Leeuwenhoek (1632–1723) made independent, groundbreaking observations of microorganisms. He used a primitive microscope designed to inspect the quality of cloth fibers to study what he described as "animalcules" swimming in a drop of water. He was able to observe a number of microorganisms, including bacteria and what was probably *Giardia*, a parasite that causes diarrhea. Observations using microscopes sparked religious and scientific fervor throughout Europe during the late seventeenth century, as people learned to accept that living creatures could be invisible to the naked eye. Although the microscope enabled visualization and study of microorganisms, little would be learned about their relationship to disease for many years to come.

The first person to suggest that microorganisms spread disease was Ignaz Semmelweis (1818–1865), who was a doctor in Vienna around 1840. At the time, it was common for doctors to perform autopsies and then deliver babies without washing their hands between procedures. He noticed that blood infections were more common in mothers whose babies were delivered by doctors than in those whose babies were delivered by midwives (who didn't also perform autopsies). He reasoned that an invisible agent was transferred from the bodies handled by the doctors in the autopsy room to mothers in the delivery room and that the invisible agent was responsible for the disease.

Louis Pasteur (1822–1895) was a brilliant microbiologist who made great contributions to the field early in its history. He performed experiments that refuted the theory of spontaneous generation of life, treated food to with heat to prevent spoilage (now known as pasteurization) and developed vaccines to prevent diseases. Most importantly, he and a scientist named Robert Koch developed the germ theory of disease. According to their theory, microorganisms cause infectious diseases and microorganisms can be isolated and differentiated in the laboratory. Robert Koch developed what are known as Koch's postulates, which are still used today to help identify the causative agent of an infectious disease. (See Table 2.1)

Table 2.1
Koch's Postulates to Demonstrate a Specific Microbial Cause of Disease

1.	The microorganism must be obtained from a diseased animal, and must be present in every animal that has the disease.
2.	The microorganism must be isolated and grown in pure culture.
3.	The cultured microorganism must be inoculated into a healthy animal, which then contracts the same disease.
4.	Identical microorganisms are recovered for the diseased animal and isolated again in pure culture.

Bacteria, fungi, and parasites were discovered soon after the invention of the microscope, but viruses were not discovered until the late 1800s. Viruses were elusive because they are so small that they are invisible even under the best conventional microscope and because the methods used to grow bacteria do not work for viruses. They were ultimately discovered when it was shown that certain liquids passed through fine, bacteria-trapping filters could still cause infections in plants. As a result, they were originally known as "filterable agents." Eventually, with the help of powerful electron microscopes and unique laboratory methods, scientists learned much more about viruses.

During the twentieth century, microbiologists learned a great deal about microorganisms and developed a variety of ways to isolate and identify them. Advances in microscope technology enabled many discoveries. Conventional microscopes were enhanced to have greater resolution and other special properties throughout the century and electron microscopes were invented in 1931. Electron microscopes are expensive and take a great deal of skill to use, but they enable detailed observations of microorganisms, including viruses. Electron microscopes are now used in many large microbiology laboratories. In addition, microbiologists in the twentieth century learned a great deal about the nutritional requirements and metabolic processes of microorganisms, which facilitated easier identification of environmental and clinical isolates and a great deal of laboratory experimentation and discovery.

Since 1980, many discoveries concerning infectious diseases and microorganisms have come from the ability to manipulate and understand the genetic information encoded in DNA. Molecular technologies now enable scientists to determine the genetic sequence of microorganisms and the significance of particular genes. A molecular technique called Polymerase Chain Reaction (PCR) has made it possible to detect microorganisms without having to culture them. This has been a boon to those who study infectious diseases because many disease-causing microorganisms cannot be grown under laboratory conditions. Now, microbiologists can search for and study microorganisms using molecular methods, conventional methods, or both, depending on the microorganism in question and other factors.

2.4 Types of Microorganisms

Infectious microorganisms are traditionally divided into four main categories: viruses, bacteria, parasites and fungi. These four categories are defined by the size, genetic makeup and mechanism of replication of the microorganism.

A. Viruses

With the exception of newly discovered prions, which are discussed later in the book, viruses are the smallest agents of infectious disease. Most viruses are exceedingly small and are essentially round in shape. They consist of little more than a small piece of genetic material surrounded by a thin coating of protein. Some viruses are also surrounded by a thin, fatty envelope. Viruses are different from all other infectious microorganisms because they are the only group of microorganisms that cannot replicate outside of a host organism. Because viruses do not eat food, but instead seize materials and energy from host cells, some scientists argue that they are more like complex molecules than living creatures. Viruses are known to infect nearly every type of organism on Earth. Some viruses, called bacteriophages, even infect bacteria.

B. Bacteria

Bacteria are ten to 100 times larger than viruses. They acquire energy from the same essential sources as humans, including sugars, proteins, and fats. Some bacteria live and multiply in the environment while others are adapted to life within human hosts. Bacteria cause many types of diseases, ranging in severity from mild skin irritation to lethal pneumonia. Most bacteria consist of a ring of DNA surrounded by cellular machinery, contained within a fatty membrane. Some bacteria can double in number every fifteen minutes while others may take weeks or months to divide and grow.

C. Parasites

Parasites are part of a large group of organisms called eukaryotes. Parasites are different from bacteria or viruses because their cells share many features with human cells including a defined nucleus. Parasites are usually larger than bacteria, although some environmentally resistant forms are nearly as small. Some parasites only replicate within a host organism, but many can multiply freely in the environment. Parasites can be made of one cell, as is the case with *Giardia*, or many cells, as is the case with parasitic worms. In developing countries, parasitic worms are a major source of disease. Waterborne, non-worm parasites, including *Giardia* and *Cryptosporidium* are most common sources of parasitic disease in the United States.

D. Fungi

Fungi are diverse in terms of their shape, size and means of infecting humans. Fungi are eukaryotes, meaning that like parasites, their cells have a true nucleus and complex internal structures. They are most commonly found as environmentally resistant spores and molds, but can cause disease in humans in the form of yeasts. Fungi most often cause skin infections and pneumonia. Fungal diseases are particularly dangerous to immunocompromised people, such as those suffering from AIDS.

2.5 Omnipresence of Microbial Life

The number of microorganisms that live on the human body is staggering. In fact, each person is home to about ten trillion microorganisms (Buckman 2002). Most live in the gut, where the vast surface area of the intestines is colonized with trillions of microorganisms. Human skin is another known repository of microorganisms. Studies have shown that between 100 and one million bacteria live on each square centimeter of skin (Larson 2003). Most bacteria are found in the wetter parts of our bodies, such as the feet, armpits, and skin around the eyes. In general, microorganisms thrive in warm, moist environments. Not surprisingly, many places within homes, food, and bodies harbor microorganisms.

Microorganisms also are ubiquitous in the environment. Despite their small size, they comprise one tenth to one third of Earth's total biomass (D'Hondt 2002). Soil, water, air, and food all abound with microorganisms. Studies suggest that fertile soil is home to approximately one billion microorganisms per gram. Even a hot, dry desert soil contains about ten million microorganisms per gram (Paul and Clark 1989). Water also contains a great number of microorganisms. The concentration of culturable bacteria in public tap water varies greatly, but is approximately one million bacteria per liter on average (Stine 2004). Municipal wastewater contains approximately 10^{12} bacteria, 1,000 viruses, and 1,000 parasites per liter (Maier et al. 2000). The air we breathe also contains appreciable concentrations of microorganisms. Indoor air contains from a few to tens of thousands of bacteria and fungi per cubic meter, depending on the building. Outdoor air typically contains higher concentrations of microorganisms, reaching into millions per cubic meter of air near agricultural operations (Tong 1999). Many types of food also are home to microorganisms. Yogurt and sour cream are given their unique flavor and texture by living, breeding bacteria and contain millions of microorganisms per spoonful. Healthy foods such as salad, fresh fruit, and bean sprouts harbor some of the highest concentrations of bacteria, ranging from 1,000,000, to 100,000,000 per gram. Food is the major source of bacteria we ingest (Stine 2004).

2.6 Pathogenic versus Non-Pathogenic Microorganisms

Microorganisms can be divided into three groups with respect to their potential to cause diseases. Those that typically cause diseases are referred to as pathogens or pathogenic microorganisms. Specific pathogens cause specific diseases. Examples are *Helicobacter pylori*, which causes gastric ulcers and influenza virus, which causes the flu. In some cases, one type of pathogen can infect different parts of the body, resulting in different diseases. Microorganisms that are capable of causing diseases but do so only under certain circumstances are called opportunistic pathogens. Opportunistic pathogens can cause diseases that are just as severe as those caused by pathogens, but opportunistic pathogens usually only infect humans whose immune systems are compromised in some way. Once an opportunistic pathogen has gained footing in a host, infection can be persistent and deadly. For example, *Pseudomonas aeruginosa* is commonly found in soil, water, and on our bodies. But this bacterium causes a severe and often deadly infection of the throat in individuals afflicted with cystic fibrosis (Rajan 2002). Microorganisms that are not known to cause diseases are referred to as commensal or non-pathogenic microorganisms. Non-pathogenic microorganisms do not cause diseases. Many non-pathogenic microorganisms simply cannot live or grow in the environment provided by the human body because they are adapted to life in environments that are scarce in nutrients or environments that are very cold, hot, salty, or dry. Other non-pathogenic microorganisms can live in the environment of the human body, but do so commensally, or without causing harm. Non-pathogenic microorganisms can benefit humans by competing with disease-causing microorganisms for space and nutrients within the human body, which provides protection from infection by pathogens.

2.7 The Immune System

The immune system functions to shield the body from pathogens encountered in the environment and protects us by recognizing and destroying pathogens and the toxins they produce. Considering the omnipresence of microbial life, the immune system's ability to protect the body from infections and degradation by microorganisms is extraordinary. The human immune system is complex and is discussed only briefly in this book. For additional reference, consider *The Immune System*, by Peter Parham (Parham 2000).

Innate immunity is the state of immunity with which one is born. It exists before exposure to a pathogen and is not enhanced by repeated exposures. Examples of innate immunity include the skin, which serves as a protective barrier against microorganisms and mucous in the respiratory tract, which traps microorganisms in the air. The outward flow of urine, tears, and blood are other innate mechanisms that help protect the body from infections. Once a pathogen has invaded the body, the innate immune system may respond with inflammation or fever.

Acquired immunity develops as a result of exposure to a foreign substance. It is specific for a particular pathogen and is enhanced by repeated exposure to that pathogen. When born, humans have very little acquired immunity. Early in life, mothers give some immunity through breast milk. Later, a number of highly specialized molecules and cells develop in the body, each of which is programmed to perform certain tasks to help recognize and kill pathogens. Antibodies are a key part of the acquired immune system. They are large molecules that recognize and bind to characteristic parts of microorganisms called antigens. Antibodies can kill pathogens or mark them for destruction by other immune cells. Macrophages and T-cells are other important components of the immune system. Macrophages are large cells that travel through the body and check other cells for microbial infections. If an infection is found, they notify T-cells that then destroy the cells for the greater good of the body. Many other specialized cells and molecules play important roles in the immune system. (See Table 2.2)

Table 2.2
Components of the Immune System and Their Function

Component	Function	Characteristics
Antibodies	Neutralize toxins, coat and inactivate pathogens, assist in killing of pathogens by immune cells	Large molecule, v-shaped, specific for particular antigens
B-Cells	Produce antibodies, establish immune memory	Complex cell, exists in an active or dormant state depending on presence of pathogen
T-Cells	Kill cells infected with pathogens or control other T-cells	Diverse group of cells, differentiated by different chemical receptors
Macrophages	Check host cells for infection, engulf and kill pathogens, and present antigens to other immune cells	Large cell, sometimes are stationary, sometimes wander throughout the body, locate pathogens by chemicals they secrete
Granulocytes	Secrete chemicals that cause inflammation, initiate immune response	Large cells, can be triggered to release chemicals like histamines when presented with appropriate antigen
Cytokines	Help immune cells communicate with one another, regulate immune response	Small molecules, commonly recognized by immune cells as chemical messengers

Vaccines take advantage of the acquired immune system's ability to remember a pathogen and protect the body from future insults with the same pathogen. There are two different types of vaccines. Active vaccines consist of weakened pathogens that are injected into a healthy person. Inside the person, the microorganisms grow slowly and may even infect some cells. During this mild infection, the immune system produces antibodies against the pathogen and readies itself for future encounters. Passive vaccines, on the other hand, include no live microorganisms. Instead, microbiologists isolate a part of a pathogen or one of its by-products, usually a toxin, and alter it chemically to render it non-toxic. When injected into a person, the immune system produces antibodies against the altered toxin that are also effective against the real toxin. Vaccines have been responsible for dramatic declines in the prevalence of many terrible diseases, such as smallpox and polio, and have proven to be so effective that children are now vaccinated against a broad range of pathogens. Unfortunately, vaccine development is challenging and vaccines have not yet been developed to prevent many important diseases.

2.8 Sequelae of Infectious Diseases

The first part of an infection is referred to as the acute phase. In most cases, the immune system clears infections during the acute phase, eliminating all symptoms of disease. However, pathogens sometimes persist in the body or cause the immune system to attack the body as if it were a microorganism. This can result in chronic, postponed, or accompanying effects of infectious diseases called sequelae. Disease sequelae may be more debilitating than the symptoms of acute infections, so it is important for lawyers and judges to be aware of them.

Many different sequelae are associated with infectious diseases. Reactive or aseptic arthritis is probably the most common chronic effect of infectious disease. Infections with *Neisseria gonorrhoea*, *E. coli*, *Shigella*, *Salmonella*, *Campylobacter*, and other bacteria can all produce arthritis. People with certain immune system make-ups can be up to 18 times more susceptible to arthritic sequelae (Yu 1994). Other sequelae from microbial infections include infertility, autoimmune thyroid disease, juvenile type 1 diabetes, inflammatory bowel disease, renal disease, and neurological or neuromuscular disorders (Lindsay 1997). As reported previously, strep throat can produce a chronic disease called rheumatoid fever, when the immune system cross-reacts with a part of the causal bacterium that resembles a protein on the heart.

Scientists poorly understand many of the long-term effects of infectious diseases. The main reason for this is that the chronic effects of infections very often resemble other diseases that are not caused by infections, making the original cause of symptoms difficult to pinpoint. As a result, some scientists suspect that some mysterious ailments like chronic fatigue syndrome may be caused by microbial infections. Links may one day be established between several infectious diseases and their chronic effects, but they are currently prohibited by cost, low rates of occurrence, and generally low feasibility of studies.

2.9 Routes of Disease Transmission

Infectious diseases are transmitted through specific media, like air, water, food, body fluid, or insects. For example, HIV is spread through body fluid and malaria is spread by insects. A few pathogens can be spread through multiple routes. Pathogens that are spread through the same medium are likely to be similar in terms of environmental resistance, magnitude of potential outbreaks, effective interventions, and reservoir in the environment. During a disease outbreak, the route of disease transmission has great bearing on the types of specimens microbiologists collect for analysis and the intervention measures they recommend.

Diseases that are normally transmitted through water are called waterborne diseases. Drinking water is the most important source of exposure to waterborne pathogens, but pathogens can also be transmitted through recreational and bathing water. On average, humans drink approximately two liters of water per day, and studies have shown that ingestion of even one viable microorganism is capable of initiating certain infections (Haas 1999). Thus, even low-level contamination of drinking water can create enormous epidemics of disease. For example, in 1993, the city of Milwaukee, WI, experienced an outbreak of the parasite *Cryptosporidium parvum*. In less than a month, more than 400,000 people were infected. More than 100 eventually died as a result of the infection. Later, scientists estimated that the concentration of the parasite in drinking water during the outbreak was around one per liter (Haas 1999). Because waterborne pathogens are a major source of disease, drinking water is disinfected prior to distribution and a slight disinfectant residual is maintained in most water distribution systems. Recreational water and bathing water are other sources of waterborne diseases. Improperly treated swimming pools and spas are well-documented sources of waterborne pathogens. In addition, infections can arise from parasites that live freely in lakes, streams or contaminated bathing water. Since environmental water bodies cannot be treated with disinfectants, efforts to keep them safe center on effective sewage treatment and disinfection.

Diseases that can be spread through contaminated food are called foodborne diseases. Foodborne diseases are a major source of disease in the United States. Foodborne diseases are caused by pathogens (usually contaminants from the feces of a food animals) growing in and damaging intestinal cells or by the action of bacterial toxins on the intestines. The most commonly implicated agents of foodborne disease are *Staphylococcus*, *Campylobacter*, *Salmonella*, *E. coli*, and norovirus. These microorganisms all cause diarrhea and a few are associated with more severe symptoms. For example, *E. coli* strain O157:H7 can cause profuse, bloody diarrhea, kidney failure, and death. Tracking the source of foodborne disease transmission is particularly challenging for microbiologists, because food may be subject to contamination from various sources before it is eaten and because samples are infrequently available for microbiological analysis by the time a foodborne disease outbreak is recognized and investigated.

Diseases that are transmitted through the air are called airborne diseases. A variety of pathogens cause airborne diseases including bacteria, viruses, and fungi. Some airborne diseases are spread from person to person. Examples of such diseases are tuberculosis and the flu, which are transmitted by bacteria in aerosols and cause millions of deaths each year (Dye 1999). Other airborne diseases are spread through contact with environmental sources of airborne pathogens. For example, the bacterium *Legionella pneumophila* can grow in hot tubs, air conditioning units, and water heaters and can infect people who inhale tiny aerosols from these sources (Tanner 2004). Many airborne pathogens have the potential to cause massive pandemics of disease. Thus, airborne diseases are a challenge to public health professionals. In addition, many pathogens that can be spread through air have the potential to be used as biological weapons.

Infectious diseases can also be transmitted by contaminated body-fluids and sexual contact. The most important diseases transmitted in this manner are HIV, and hepatitis B and C. The most notable fluid-borne pathogen is HIV; at least 20 million people have died as a result of HIV and 5 million new HIV infections occurred in 2004 alone (UNAIDS 2004). Control measures for fluid-borne diseases center on using condoms, combating intravenous drug abuse, and screening blood banks for bloodborne pathogens.

Diseases can also be spread by biting or stinging insects. In the United States, Lyme disease and West Nile Virus infections are spread by contact with insects. Malaria, which is caused by a parasite transmitted by mosquitoes, is the third leading cause of death from infectious disease worldwide, behind HIV and tuberculosis. Insect-borne diseases are not a major problem in the United States.

2.10 Economic Impact of Infectious Diseases

Infectious diseases are expensive to individuals because of costs associated with medical treatment and lost productivity. Only a small percentage of infected people ultimately seek professional medical attention. For those who do, specimens may need to be collected for laboratory analysis to aid in diagnosis and antimicrobial drugs may be prescribed for treatment. For serious infections, hospitalization may be required along with medical procedures to mitigate damage done to the body by infections. For example, someone with a serious *Staphylococcus* infection of the skin may have dead tissue around the infection removed surgically. The costs associated with medical treatments are clearly stated on medical bills, but other costs associated with lost productivity may be more difficult to quantify. This is important, because infections are highly associated with lost productivity.

The cost to an individual from an infectious disease may be useful information for litigation. Individual costs of infection vary widely depending on the type and severity of the disease and the effectiveness of treatment. Since infections can take many different courses, the best way to determine the cost to an individual from an infection is through medical bills, income potential, and the necessity of long-term treatment.

A few studies have estimated the aggregate costs of infections in the United States. For example, the Economic Research Service of the United States Department of Agriculture estimated disease costs associated with the common foodborne pathogens *Campylobacter*, *Salmonella*, *E. coli* and *Listeria* at 6.9 billion dollars per year, including medical costs, productivity losses, and costs of premature deaths (USDA-ERS 2004). The total cost of hospital-acquired infections is approximately 6.7 billion dollars per year in the United States (Graves 2004). Studies of the cost of infectious diseases suggest that they are a major financial burden.

2.11 Chapter Summary

Microorganisms are ubiquitous in our environment and consist of viruses, bacteria, parasites and fungi. Although there are many microorganisms, only a relatively small number are capable of causing disease in otherwise healthy individuals. Microorganisms that usually cause infections are called pathogens. Pathogens that tend to cause disease in immunocompromised people are called opportunistic pathogens. Microorganisms that do not cause diseases are called non-pathogens and may live commensally in or on the body. The immune system protects the body from infections by microorganisms. Innate immunity is provided through physical barriers and mechanical processes, such as our skin and the outward flow of tears, blood, and urine. Acquired immunity is provided through the action of antibodies and a range of specialized cells that recognize and destroy foreign matter in the body. Some infections are associated with prolonged, chronic, or seemingly unrelated side effects called sequelae that may be mediated by the immune system or brought about by prolonged infections. Infectious diseases are expensive because of medical treatment costs and lost productivity.

Chapter 3

Biology of Microorganisms: The Fundamentals for Lawyers and Judges

Synopsis

3.1 Chapter Preview

This chapter educates lawyers and judges about the fundamental physical properties and life cycles of microorganisms and can be used as a reference during litigation. In this chapter, nature's vast collection of microorganisms is broken into six groups: bacteria, viruses, parasites, fungi, viroids, and prions. Helpful generalizations about microorganisms are presented first. Then, for each group, life cycles and notable characteristics of the microorganisms are explained. By reading this chapter, legal professionals will gain a practical understanding of the fundamental qualities of infectious disease agents, without wasting time on unimportant details or being daunted by the breadth of information available.

3.2 Introduction

A man carries his medical records into a lawyer's office, visibly upset. He explains that he wishes to sue his neighbor because he believes his neighbor is responsible for his recurring viral infections. He claims that viruses are growing and multiplying in his neighbor's stagnant pond and making him ill by leaching into his well, which is nearby. Doctors report that the man has recently been infected with three different viruses on three separate occasions. The lawyer, interested in infectious disease, considers his case. It sounds reasonable: filthy pond, viruses growing in the muck, so she decides to take the case.

Unfortunately, by neglecting to first consider the science behind the man's claim, the lawyer accepted a dead-end case. Viruses simply cannot replicate outside of a human host, which means that no viruses are "growing" in the pond. In fact, viruses tend to die-off in stagnant water. Unless the pond was somehow receiving raw sewage, the man's infections probably came from some other source.

A basic understanding of the physical characteristics and life cycles of microorganisms is essential to any attorney seeking to make an impact in infectious disease litigation. Knowledge of the science facilitates clear and accurate discussions about microorganisms and enables attorneys to craft scientifically valid arguments.

3.3 Helpful Generalizations

It can be said that there is an exception to every rule of microbiology. That aside, generalizations are useful even to expert microbiologists because they provide a framework that allows one to navigate through the wealth of information scientists have learned about microorganisms over the last few decades. A 'roadmap' of generalizations helps those who are new to the study of microorganisms avoid common mistakes like confusing the physiological properties of one group of microorganisms with that of another. In fact, introductory collegiate microbiology courses predominantly teach generalizations. The following list summarizes common generalizations that are relevant to pathogens.

- From smallest to largest, microorganisms can be listed as prions, viroids, viruses, bacteria, fungi, and parasites.
- Viruses do not consume food and cannot replicate outside of a host organism's cells.
- Bacteria grow exponentially (by splitting in two repeatedly); many can grow under harsh conditions, including very hot, cold, dry, and salty environments.

- In a closed system (such as a bottle of milk left out of the refrigerator), bacteria multiply slowly at first, then rapidly, then cease multiplication, then die slowly.
- Natural phenomena, such as drying, sunlight, heat and freezing kill microorganisms over time.
- Microorganisms can be detected in many ways, including growing them in the laboratory and using molecular techniques to detect their DNA.
- Exposure to as few as one parasite or virus can result in infection, but exposure to hundreds or thousands of bacteria is usually needed to cause an infection.
- Antibiotics are special compounds that damage one specific structure or process within a microbe. Disinfectants, like bleach, damage microorganisms as a whole, destroying many parts at once.
- Over time, microorganisms develop resistance to antibiotics by natural selection, but rarely become resistant to disinfectants.
- Koch's postulates (See Table 1.2) help to identify the microbial cause of a disease.

3.4 Bacteria

Physical Characteristics and Classification

Bacteria come in four basic shapes. (Figure 3.1) Spherical bacteria are called coccoid, like *Streptococcus pyogenes*, the cause of strep throat. Elongated or rod-shaped bacteria are called bacilli, like *Escherichia coli*. Slightly curved bacteria are called vibrio, like the bacteria that cause gastric ulcers, *Helicobacter pylori*. Corkscrew shaped bacteria are called spirochete, like *Treponema pallidum*, the cause of syphilis. If a bacterium is less tightly wound than spirochetes, they are called spirilli. Bacteria that can assume many shapes are called pleomorphic.

Bacteria are very small and the general rule is that bacteria are larger than viruses but smaller than parasites or fungi. They range in size from approximately 0.2 to 5.0 micrometers (μm) in length. This means that bacteria are only visible with the aid of a microscope and they can pass through porous materials such as fabrics or loosely packed soil. Because they are so small, bacteria aren't noticeable in liquids until they reach concentrations of greater than around one million bacteria per drop.

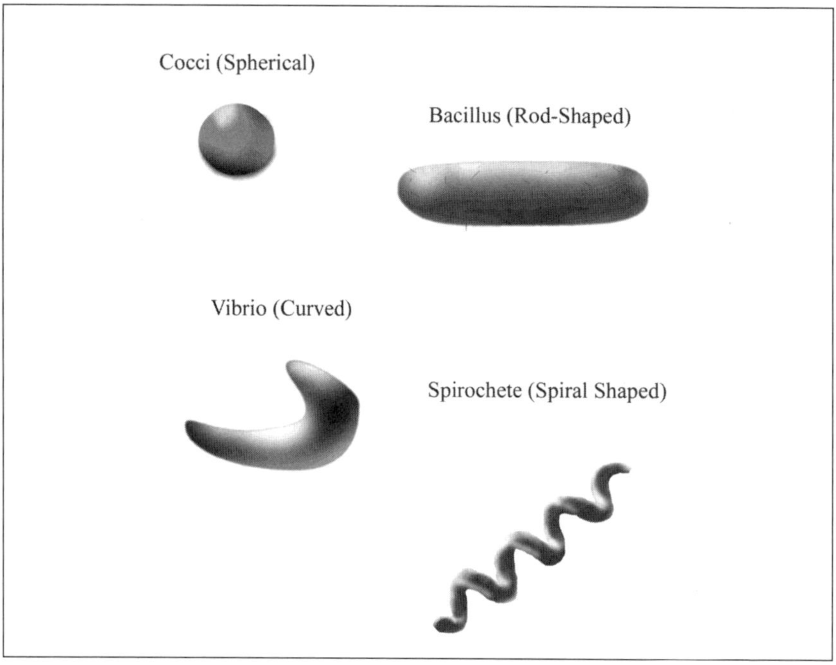

Figure 3.1 *Shapes of bacteria.*

As Figure 3.2 shows, bacteria usually consist of a cell wall, a fatty membrane, a collection of genetic material and various external structures. The salty liquid interior of a bacterium is called the protoplasm and can be thought of as the bacterium's blood. Bacterial cell walls provide them with rigidity that helps resist swelling or shrinking that can occur during changes in the saltiness, or osmotic pressure, of the bacterial environment. Bacterial membranes allow them to selectively move nutrients into the cell from the environment and to exclude harmful matter from the cell. DNA serves as the bacterium's genetic blueprint, and is condensed as a large, circular chromosome inside of the bacterial membrane. In addition to the bacterial chromosome, bacteria can also carry small loops of DNA known as plasmids, which enable bacteria to make toxins or resist antibiotics. Plasmids are easily transferred from one bacterium to another. Many bacteria also have tiny hair-like structures called flagella, which are used for locomotion. In addition to these features, some bacteria secrete slime to protect them from environmental degradation and harsh chemicals and to help them adhere to surfaces.

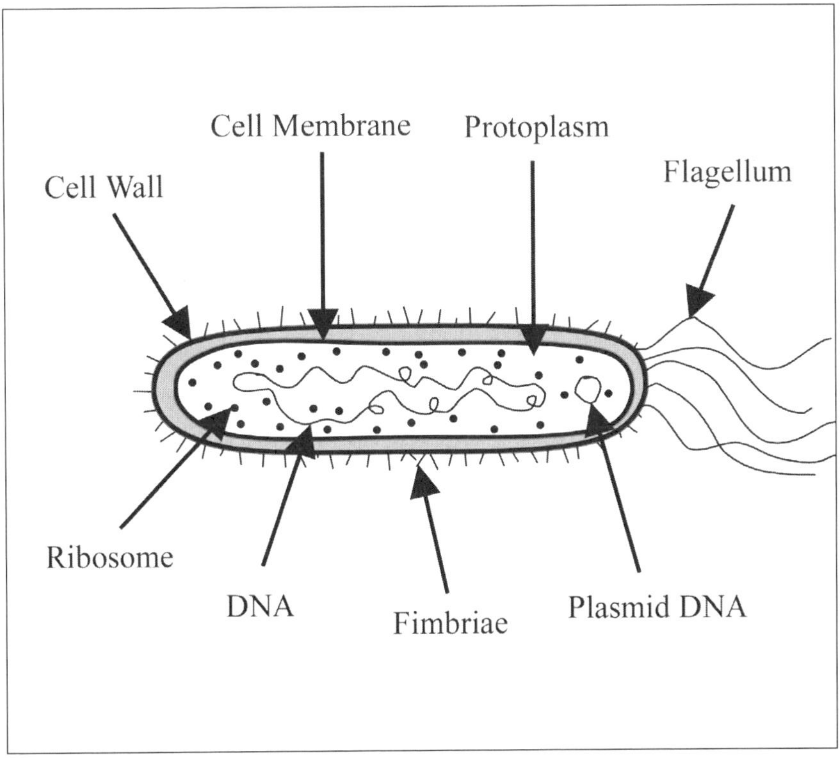

Figure 3.2 *Compoents of a bacterium.*

Some bacteria are able to encapsulate themselves in a hard coating, called a spore, under stressful environmental conditions. These bacteria are called spore-formers. *Bacillus anthracis*, the causative agent of anthrax, is an example of a spore-former. Inside protective spores, bacteria can withstand extreme temperatures, low relative humidity, ultraviolet radiation and the action of common disinfectants. When conditions are suitable for growth, the spore swells and breaks, allowing the bacterium to multiply once again.

Life Cycle

Bacteria multiply by splitting from one into two cells in a process known as binary fission. In most cases, the rate of growth of bacteria is controlled by temperature. Bacteria tend to replicate slowly when refrigerated and rapidly when incubated at higher temperatures. Bacteria of public health concern tend to grow most rapidly near the temperature of the human body. High temperatures (above 160 ^{0}F) inactivate most bacteria.

As Figure 3.3 shows, bacterial growth in the presence of excess nutrients follows a standard growth curve consisting of a lag phase, an exponential phase, a plateau phase and a death phase. During the lag phase, bacteria adjust to their surroundings and prepare to grow. The duration of the lag phase depends on the environment. In laboratory cultures or in the human body the lag phase is brief, but in nutrient-poor environments the lag phase may last for weeks or months. After the lag phase, bacteria enter the exponential phase, where they grow and divide rapidly. Population increases by bacteria during the exponential phase can be impressive. For example, one *E. coli* bacterium can turn into one billion overnight. When bacteria have expended the majority of nutrients within a system, they enter the plateau phase, where they reach equilibrium between factors preventing growth and factors enabling growth. As a result, the total number of bacteria remains constant. Some bacteria drastically reduce the rate at which they metabolize during the plateau phase, allowing them to survive for long periods of time under these circumstances. After some time, bacteria enter the death phase. During this phase some bacteria may still be growing but there is a net loss in population. One cause of microbial death during the death phase is the accumulation of toxic growth by-products in the culture, which may be acidic or may damage critical components of the bacteria. In the setting of the human body, bacteria usually enter the death phase as a result of pressure from the immune system.

3.5 Viruses

Physical Characteristics and Classification

With the exception of prions and viriods, which are not fully understood, viruses are the smallest agents of infectious disease. Viruses are about ten times smaller than bacteria, ranging in size from about 20 to 250 nanometers (nm). At this size, viruses are invisible under light microscopes. Viruses are so small that they are only visible with the aid of electron microscopes.

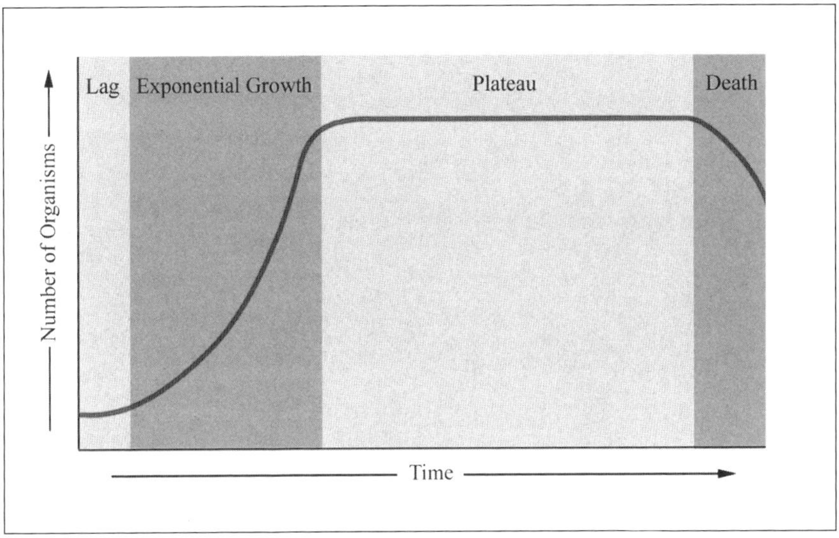

Figure 3.3 *Standard Bacterial Growth Curve.*

Viruses have unique, dense structures. They consist of genetic material, in the form of DNA or RNA, surrounded by a thin layer of protein. (Figure 3.4) A fatty envelope also surrounds some viruses. Unlike bacteria, viruses do not contain liquid. Viruses also display unique protein structures externally, which enable them to bind to or interact with host cells.

Viruses are grouped into families according to their basic physical structure, genetic makeup, and life cycle. Picornaviruses, which include poliovirus and hepatitis A virus, are an example of a family of viruses. Picornaviruses are all small, round, structured viruses that contain genetic material in the form of RNA. Different viruses within the same family may infect different host animals or be spread through different disease transmission routes. Some viruses can infect more than one host animal. For example, rabies virus is known to infect humans, dogs and other animals. Different types of viruses can infect the same part of the body. For example, hepatitis A, B, and C viruses are all members of different families but all infect the liver.

Life Cycle

Viruses are unique because they do not require food and because they cannot replicate outside of the cells of another organism. They are also unique because they are the only type of microorganism that can infect all other types of microorganisms.

Although there are many different types of viruses, most replicate in the same basic fashion. First, viruses adhere to a host cell using external binding structures. In some cases, the host cell actively envelops the virus and draws it inside. In other cases, the virus injects its genetic material in the form of DNA or RNA directly into the cell. After the virus or portion thereof has entered the cell, the cell recognizes the genetic material as if it were its own. The host cell then manufactures viral proteins encoded on the viral DNA or RNA and makes copies of the viral genetic material that was originally taken into the cell. These materials then come together in shells made of viral proteins called capsids. After replication, some viruses simply burst out of the cell, while others, such as HIV and the virus that causes Sudden Acute Respiratory Syndrome (SARS), bud slowly from the cell, becoming encapsulated in a fatty envelope.

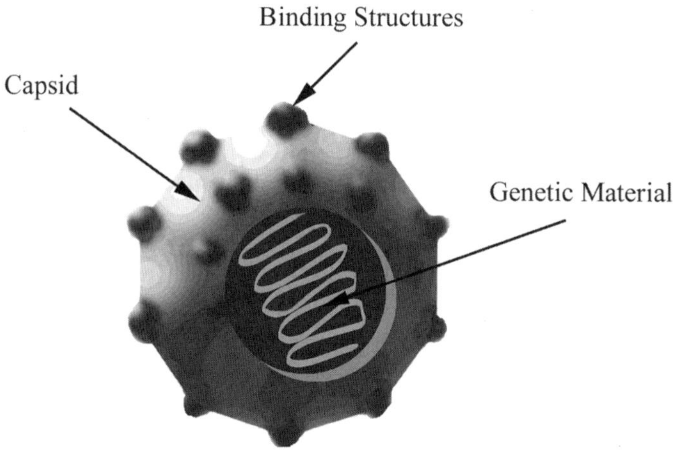

Figure 3.4 *Components of a virus.*

After viruses are released from infected cells, they exit the body through some body-fluid. All body-fluids can harbor viruses, including blood, urine and saliva. To facilitate survival of progeny, large quantities of viruses are often released into the environment. In the case of rotavirus, where one virus can initiate infection, up to 10^{10} have been reported in the feces of an infected person (White and Fenner 1994).

3.6 Parasites

Physical Characteristics and Classification

Parasites can be microscopic or visible to the naked eye, depending on the type of parasite. Smaller parasites, such as the waterborne parasites *Giardia lamblia* and *Cyrptosporidium parvum*, are never large enough to see without a microscope. However, intestinal worms, like tapeworms, may grow to be several feet long and can be viewed with the naked eye.

For the purpose of this book, parasites are defined as disease causing, eukaryotic (nucleus-having) microorganisms excluding fungi. Parasites contain more evolutionarily advanced cellular structures than bacteria and store cellular components within distinct membrane-enclosed structures called organelles. Some parasites are composed of one cell while others are composed of many.

Life Cycle

The life cycles of many parasites are complicated, often involving multiple intermediate forms and different animal hosts. For example, the life cycle of some human parasites involves infection of snails, humans and insect larvae. However, most parasites have one thing in common: some type of microscopic, environmentally resistant form that is associated with disease transmission. For parasitic diseases relevant to developed countries, the environmentally resistant form (called a cyst, oocyst, or ova) is usually ingested as a contaminant in food or water. After ingestion, the parasites begin to grow and multiply in the gut. In most cases, the parasite simply produces more environmentally resistant forms, which are expelled in feces. Some parasites, however, can migrate to other body tissues after ingestion, such as the lungs or brain.

Parasitic worms are a major source of disease in developing countries. However, in the developed world the overall burden of infection by such worms is low. This is primarily a result of the impact that advanced wastewater treatment has on the life cycle of parasitic worms (Maier 2000).

3.7 Fungi

Physical Characteristics and Classification

Fungi are eukaryotic (nucleus-having) microorganisms that range in size from microscopic to macroscopic. In soil, single fungal colonies have been reported to spread over several acres (Maier et al. 2000). Some fungi can grow in a unicellular form called a yeast. Yeasts resemble large bacteria, except they contain more advanced cellular components. Fungi tend to grow as molds in the outdoor environment and on skin. When growing as molds, they produce hyphae, which are the tiny hair-like structures that can be observed on moldy bread or fruit. When growing as molds, fungi use spores to reproduce. Spores are usually microscopic, but some are large enough to be seen with the unaided eye.

Many fungi can be identified by their phenotype, or external features, after being grown on a nutrient medium so that they produce both hyphae and spores. Microbiologists then stain the fungus and use a microscope to compare its features with drawings of various species of fungi on a reference chart. Identification of fungi in this manner may be difficult or may even require an expert in fungi, called a mycologist. Alternatively, microbiologists may look for specific sequences of DNA to identify fungi by using molecular techniques.

Life Cycle

Many fungi are dimorphic, meaning that they can grow either as yeasts or molds depending on environmental factors. For fungi growing as molds, life starts when a spore germinates in an environment suitable for growth. As the fungus grows, it produces hair-like hyphae that penetrate the surrounding area to absorb nutrients. As growth continues, the fungus produces spores, which are spread to surrounding environments through air. Many fungi can also grow as yeasts. Yeasts usually grow in liquids and behave like bacteria with respect to the standard growth curve. Unlike bacteria, which divide by splitting in two, yeasts multiply by budding. During budding, a small yeast begins to grow as a part of the outside of a mature yeast cell. When it is large enough, the smaller cell separates itself, and carries on the process of growing and producing progeny.

Fungi play an important role in natural systems because they are very good at obtaining food from nutrient-poor environments. In the setting of infectious disease, fungi are successful because they are highly adaptive to the environmental stresses encountered in and around the human body, such as on skin that is alternatively wet and then dry.

3.8 Viroids and Prions

Viroids are the smallest infectious agents known. The role that viroids play in human disease is unknown. However, viroids are important plant pathogens that can have devastating effects on agriculture. Viroids are essentially a naked cluster of the genetic material RNA. Theoretically, viroids are taken inadvertently into a host cell, which copies the RNA and releases new viroids into the environment.

Prions are small proteins that are believed to replicate within neural tissues such as the brain and spinal cord, although they lack genetic material. Scientists theorize that disease can be transmitted from infected animals to humans by ingestion of meat contaminated with prion-containing neural tissues. The most commonly observed prion diseases include scrapie in sheep, bovine spongiform encephalopathy in cattle and Creutzfeldt-Jacob Disease (CJD) in humans (Brock 2000). All prion diseases lead to spasms and general neural degeneration, eventually resulting in death. No cures are known for any of the diseases caused by prions. Because prions are stable at high temperatures, cooking of prion-infected food does not reduce the risk of disease.

3.9 Chapter Summary

Infectious disease agents come in a variety of shapes and sizes and have markedly different life cycles. Bacteria are ubiquitous in the environment and are characterized by their small size, ability to reproduce quickly through fission, and metabolic processes. Viruses are very small microorganisms that lack the ability to metabolize food or replicate outside of host cells. Although there are many types of viruses, they all replicate in the same basic fashion that involves adhesion to a host cell, invasion of the cell, replication within the cell, and expulsion from the cell. Parasites are a diverse group of eukaryotic (nucleus-having) microorganisms that have complex life cycles and share an environmentally resistant stage that is similar to a microscopic egg. Fungi are unique microorganisms that are also eukaryotic and can exist as either yeasts or molds, depending on environmental circumstances. They are typically classified on the basis of their appearance under a microscope in the form of spores or mold. Viroids are naked clusters of RNA that are important agricultural pathogens. Prions are self-replicating proteins that appear to be transmitted from food animals to humans by ingestion.

Chapter 4

Virulence and Antibiotic Resistance

Synopsis

4.1 Chapter Preview

This chapter introduces the concept of virulence, which is the combination of a microorganism's ability to colonize and invade the body and its ability to produce dangerous toxins. Antibiotic resistance is also discussed. This chapter will help lawyers and judges understand the factors that set an ordinary germ apart from a devastating pathogen.

4.2 Introduction

People rarely sue over mild infections, like colds caused by seasonal viruses, no matter how negligent transmission of the disease may have been. Litigation is much more likely to occur when infections result in serious illness. The severity of an infection depends on the virulence of the pathogen. Thus, lawyers and judges can benefit from understanding the factors that contribute to microbial virulence.

Virulence can be thought of as the combination of a microorganism's ability to invade and grow within tissues and its ability to exude toxins. The virulence of a virus is defined by its ability to invade and replicate within cells, because viruses lack the machinery needed to produce toxins. Some bacteria, such as *Salmonella*, produce at least three separate classes of toxins. Fungi are also known to produce toxins. *Stachybotyrs chartarum* is one such example. It secretes a potent neurological toxin, which is speculated to contribute to indoor air contamination (Hossain 2004).

Although antibiotic resistance is not a classical virulence factor, it is now a major factor in the severity and outcome of many infections. Since current treatments for bacterial infections depend largely on antibiotics, infections by antibiotic resistant bacteria are usually more persistent and damaging than other infections. Antibiotic resistance comes about in many ways, but is generally driven by low levels of antibiotics used in animal feed and by frequent usage of antibiotics to treat infections. Much like the genes that encode toxins, the genes that encode antibiotic resistance can be spread from bacterium to bacterium on small loops of DNA called plasmids. Certain viruses, like HIV, can develop resistance to specialized antiviral drugs.

4.3 Adhesion and Invasion Factors

Many virulent microorganisms are equipped with special external structures that help them bind to host cells, known as adhesion factors. Common adhesion factors include pili and fimbriae, which are hair-like structures found on some bacteria. Adhesion factors are strongly associated with virulence. The ability to adhere to cells is normally specific to certian parts of the body. For example, sexually transmitted microorganisms are known to adhere strongly to urethral and reproductive tissues, while adhering less strongly to skin tissue. Often, the particular type of adhesion factor is specified as part of the strain name of a virulent pathogen to set it apart from other bacteria of the same species. It is thought that adhesion factors dictate where microorganisms can initiate infection.

Many virulent microorganisms have developed mechanisms to invade the cells of a host organism, called invasion factors. Invasion factors vary from microorganism to microorganism. Some invasion factors simply trick host cells into thinking that they should bring bacteria inside. Other invasion factors provide microorganisms with a way to reside in host cells without being destroyed or detected by the immune system. For example, the bacteria *Staphylococcus aureus* produces compounds called carotenoids that quench antibacterial chemicals secreted by immune cells. Cellular invasion often results in fever, tissue inflammation, and pain.

4.4 Toxins

Toxins are molecules produced by microorganisms that cause damage to host cells. There are three types of toxins: exotoxins, enterotoxins and endotoxins. Different toxins play different roles in disease initiation and transmission. Some toxins disrupt the cell membrane to help microorganisms gain access to valuable nutrients within the host cell. Some toxins have systemic effects on the body and serve to confuse or overwhelm the immune system. Other toxins, such as those that cause profuse diarrhea, help to disperse microorganisms into the environment.

Exotoxins are toxins that are secreted by microorganisms that damage areas other than the intestines. Exotoxins can cause damage to host cells in the immediate vicinity of the infection or can be carried through the bloodstream to other sites within the body. Exotoxins are the main source of virulence for some strains of microorganisms. For example, most *Staphylococcus* bacteria are normal, non-pathogenic inhabitants of humans. However, one species, called *Staphylococcus aureus*, secretes a toxin that disrupts host cell membranes. The dramatic effect of this toxin can be seen when *Staphylococcus aureus* is grown on a medium containing intact red blood cells. As the bacterium grows and produces the toxin, the blood cells in the agar burst, rendering a clear zone on the growth medium. There are many different exotoxins. Two examples are tetanus toxin secreted by *Clostridium tetani* and botulinum toxin secreted by *Clostridium botulinum*. Tetanus toxin binds to the part of nerve cells that prevents nerve impulses from being transmitted, which leads to lockjaw and eventually rigid paralysis of the entire body. Conversely, botulinum toxin blocks the release of chemicals in nerves that are required for stimulation. As a result, those exposed to botulinum toxin gradually become incapable of movement and breathing. Other exotoxins cause neurotoxicity, skin blistering, and skin irritation. Most exotoxins do not cause fever (Madigan 2000).

Enterotoxins are toxins that are secreted by microorganisms that grow in the small intestine. Enterotoxins cause intestinal cells to pump large quantities of fluid into the intestines, resulting in diarrhea. Cholera toxin is a well-studied enterotoxin. The effect of this toxin is so profound that victims often die from dehydration caused by profuse toxin-induced diarrhea. Many other bacteria secrete enterotoxins, including *Staphylococcus aureus*, *Salmonella*, *Campylobacter*, *Shigella*, and various strains of *E. coli*.

Endotoxins are another type of toxin. Endotoxins are unique because bacteria do not secrete them. Rather, endotoxins are a part of the surface of gram-negative bacteria called a lipopolysaccharide. Endotoxins are far less toxic than exotoxins. Nevertheless, they can cause fever, diarrhea, and even shock if exposure is extreme. Because endotoxins can cause fever, levels are monitored in pharmaceuticals. Although they are technically toxins, endotoxins are treated more like irritants outside of the medical arena. They are normally present at high levels in the environment and are released when gram-negative bacteria are destroyed or die naturally. Exposure to endotoxin from environmental sources is normally not sufficient to cause disease. However, indoor waste handlers and certain agricultural workers sometimes develop respiratory diseases after excessive exposure.

4.5 Gene Transfer and the DNA Plasmid

The genes that encode exotoxins, enterotoxins, and antibiotic resistance are frequently transferred from one bacterium to another on small loops of DNA called plasmids. A plasmid is simply a small loop of DNA that exists outside of the bacterial chromosome and contains genes that allow the bacterium to perform a specific function. DNA plasmids can encode degradative enzymes, resistance to antibiotics, resistance to metals, resistance to bacteriophage infection, and various other physiological functions (Pepper 1994). Such transfer of virulence can occur inside of infected hosts or between bacteria in the environment (Kruse 1994). Virulence factors also can be transferred to bacteria when they are infected with certain viruses, called bacteriophages. Gene transfer can have a major impact on microbial virulence.

Bacteria acquire new genes in three ways. Bacterial conjugation is the most important mechanism. During conjugation, bacteria are physically conjoined by a hollow tube called a pilus. The donor bacterium, which may or may not be of the same species as the recipient, transfers genetic material to the recipient in the form of a DNA plasmid. Donor bacteria have may have multiple copies of the plasmid, so transfer of the genetic material does not necessarily reduce the donor's virulence. Many conjugation events are mediated by conjugation-programmed plasmids themselves. Genes can also be transferred between bacteria through transformation. Transformation occurs when bacteria take in DNA from their environment. This can happen when bacteria of one species are grown in the presence of dead bacteria from another species. The last mechanism of gene transfer is gene transduction. Gene transduction occurs when genetic material is transferred between bacteria by bacteriophages. Transduction can have a dramatic effect on virulence. For example, *Corynebacterium diphtheriae*, the bacteria that causes diphtheria, is non-pathogenic until it has been infected with bacteriophage β. After infection, the bacterium is able to produce diphtheria toxin, which is a potent exotoxin that kills epithelial cells in the throat and can lead to airway blockage and death.

4.6 Antibiotics and Antibiotic Resistance

It is important to recognize the difference between antibiotics and antiseptics or disinfectants. Antibiotics are drugs used to cure infections by inactivating specific components of bacteria. In contrast, disinfectants and antiseptics are chemicals used outside of the body to rid surfaces of microbial contaminants. Since disinfectants and antiseptics attack many parts of bacteria at once, whereas antibiotics attack one specific component, it is usually much easier for a microorganism to adapt to damage caused by an antibiotic than from a chemical disinfectant. For this reason, many bacteria have become resistant to antibiotics, but resistance to disinfectants has not yet been observed.

Resistance to antibiotics among microorganisms is increasing rapidly and is a major threat to public health. Antibiotic resistance has now been observed in one bacterium or another against every common antibiotic, including the powerful antibiotic Vancomycin. Resistance of bacteria to antibiotics has increased steadily since penicillin began to be used to treat diseases and since antibiotics were introduced into animal feed at low levels to enhance growth. No one really knows whether the major cause of antibiotic resistance is clinical or agricultural use of antibiotics. Nevertheless, antibiotic resistance is redefining medical treatment regimens, raising medical costs associated with infections, and increasing the likelihood that infections will be fatal.

Antibiotic resistance among bacteria varies from strain to strain. Some microorganisms show no resistance to antibiotics. Others may be resistant to one or a few specific antibiotics but may be sensitive to the rest. Some bacteria, such as Vancomycin resistant *Staphylococcus aureus*, are resistant to virtually all antibiotics. A bacterium's ability to survive in the presence of antibiotics is determined by the general physical makeup of the microorganism and more importantly by the genes it possesses. One of the most effective mechanisms used by bacteria to defend against antimicrobial drugs is to secrete matter that binds and sequesters antibiotics.

Specific resistance mechanisms vary depending on an antibiotic's mode of action. The β-lactam antibiotics, which include penicillins and cephalosporins, bind to components of the bacterial cell wall during construction and maintenance and weaken it. Resistance to penicillins and cephalosporins can be conferred by active export of the drug away from the microorganism, by penicillin destroying proteins, and by mutations that prevent penicillin from binding to the cell wall. Sulfa drugs are another type of antibiotic. Sulfa drugs mimic a chemical that microorganisms need to produce a specific vitamin. Resistance to sulfa drugs has been widely reported and developed when bacteria acquired the ability to obtain the vitamin from outside sources. Macrolides, aminoglycosides and tetracycline are other classes of antibiotics that are similar in terms of function and the mechanisms by which they are defeated by resistant bacteria. Erythromycin, spiramycin, streptomycin, kanamycin, gentamicin, and tetracycline all belong to one of these three groups. They inhibit bacterial protein synthesis by binding to protein production sites within bacteria. Resistance to the drugs is brought about by minor changes in the structure of the protein production sites or by decreased permeation of the antibiotic into the bacterium. Quinolones are a popular class of antibiotics that include the clinically relevant drug ciprofloxacin. Quinolones kill bacteria by binding to a particular enzyme required for DNA synthesis. Resistance to quinolones can develop in bacteria that have altered the structure or function of the enzyme that synthesizes DNA.

4.7 Antiviral Drugs

Fewer antiviral drugs have been developed than antibacterial drugs because viruses are generally more costly to study in the laboratory, they have fewer targets that can be affected by drugs and because antiviral drugs frequently have high toxicity due to the intimate association between viruses and the cells they infect. Specifically, many antiviral drugs inhibit viral DNA synthesis, which can have negative effects on normal host cell DNA synthesis.

Different antiviral drugs work in different ways. Nucleoside analog antiviral drugs are building blocks for DNA that have been altered to make them defective. When incorporated into viral DNA, they prevent replication of the virus. Examples of nucleoside analog drugs include Acyclovir, which is effective against herpes viruses and Zidovudine (AZT), which helps to control HIV replication. Because of cross-reactivity with human DNA synthesis, some nucleoside inhibitors can be toxic to humans. Viral protease inhibitors are antiviral agents that function by binding to the viral enzyme responsible for finishing the production of viral proteins. Examples of protease inhibitors include Indinavir and Ritonavir, which help to control the replication of HIV. One of the most interesting antiviral agents is called interferon. Interferon is produced by the human body as a natural response to viral infections. When pure interferon is delivered into the body as a medicine, it can help to prevent the progression of certain viral diseases including chronic viral hepatitis.

The onset of AIDS in HIV-infected individuals could be controlled at one time using only nucleoside analog antiviral drugs. However, as a result of HIV's high mutation rate, a multi-drug cocktail consisting of at least three separate classes of antiviral agents is now needed to reduce viral replication. Unfortunately, even when three different drugs are used at once, HIV occasionally develops resistance and can pass this resistance on to its progeny. Therefore, it is now possible for victims to begin an infection with multi-drug resistant HIV.

4.8 Chapter Summary

Virulent microorganisms are the most common type of microorganism involved in litigation because they produce the most damage to the human body during the progression of disease. Virulence can be described as a microorganism's ability to colonize and invade the body in combination with its potential to produce toxins. Exotoxins, endotoxins, enterotoxins, fimbriae, and pili are all virulence factors. In addition, many microorganisms have become resistant to antibiotics, which makes them more dangerous. Mechanisms of antibiotic resistance vary depending on the mechanism of action of the drug and the type of microorganism. Some microorganisms are resistant to virtually all antibiotics. A few drugs have been developed against viruses, but they may be toxic and are not always effective. HIV infections are best managed using combinations of antiviral drugs to reduce the likelihood that the virus will evolve resistance.

Chapter 5

The Indicator Concept

Synopsis

5.1 Chapter Preview

This chapter discusses the relationship between certain microorganisms, called indicator microorganisms, and pathogens in the environment. Indicator microorganisms can be used to assess the microbiological quality of a system without looking for pathogens directly. Microbiologists have been using indicator microorganisms for decades with various benefits and drawbacks. Legal professionals who understand how indicator microorganisms behave in the environment relative to their pathogenic counterparts will have a clearer idea of what detection of them, or lack thereof, means during infectious disease litigation.

5.2 Introduction

Microbiologists frequently look for special bacteria and viruses called indicator microorganisms as a sign of pathogenic microorganisms in the environment. This approach has many advantages because tests for pathogens in the environment are often tedious, organism-specific, and expensive. Tests for indicator microorganisms, on the other hand, are inexpensive, require fewer reagents, and are relatively easy to perform. As a result, most environmental monitoring for pathogens is done using indicator microorganisms, which are normally much more numerous in the environment than their pathogenic counterparts.

The use of non-pathogenic microorganisms to indicate the presence of infectious agents in the environment is endorsed by the United States Government in environmental laws designed to reduce the risk of infections from environmental sources. For example, the Safe Drinking Water Act specifies that zero coliform bacteria be present in a 100 milliliter sample of drinking water. The Clean Water Act specifies that levels of fecal coliform bacteria remain below 200 cells per 100 milliliters in wastewater treatment plant effluent. Many states and municipalities require regular tests for indicator microorganisms from a variety of environmental sources including water near beaches and sewage sludge.

There can be major drawbacks to using indicator microorganisms to predict the presence or concentration of pathogens in the environment. The most significant drawback is that tests for indicator microorganisms may be negative even though pathogens may be present in great numbers. This can result in diseases being transmitted in environments thought to be safe. Conversely, detection of indicator microorganisms in cases where pathogens are absent can result in needless alarm and economic losses.

Another drawback associated with the use of indicator microorganisms is that the general public does not understand the difference between pathogens and the indicator microorganisms that suggest their presence. One of the most common misunderstandings comes from detection of *E. coli* in food, water, or air. Because of widely publicized outbreaks of a highly pathogenic strain of *E. coli* (strain O157:H7) at a fast-food restaurant chain, most people think that all *E. coli* are capable of causing deadly diseases. However, pathogenic *E. coli* are different from helpful *E. coli* in that they have the ability to produce potent toxins and are relatively rare. In fact, humans harbor trillions of helpful *E. coli* in the intestines. Nevertheless, the media frequently implies that the non-pathogenic indicator microorganisms themselves pose a risk to health. The following scenario illustrates the potential fallout from confusion about indicator microorganisms and the pathogens with which they are associated:

> A young lady, concerned about staying healthy and motivated by advertising at a large home and hardware store purchases a "home water test-kit." The package guarantees that the product will "detect deadly *E. coli*

> bacteria in drinking water in just 24 hours." She uses the kit and is terrified when the test water from her kitchen sink turns bright blue, indicating that the water is contaminated. She calls her local water utility to warn them of the threat, but they do not respond. Worried, she seeks legal advice, and pays a lawyer to look into the matter. Ultimately, she learns the distinction between indicator *E. coli* and pathogenic *E. coli* and finds that her fears were unwarranted.

In this case, time and money was wasted and a person suffered emotionally because of the misunderstanding perpetrated by the news media and public.

5.3 Criteria for Indicator Microorganisms

Certain traits define an ideal indicator microorganism. Ideally, an indicator microorganism is useful for a number of environments. It shares the same origin as its pathogenic counterpart. It is indicative of the presence of all pathogens from a particular source. It has a reasonably longer survival time than the hardiest pathogen. It does not grow in the environment and is easy to isolate and culture. Lastly, the density of the ideal indicator microorganism is related, in some way, to the concentration of the pathogen in the environment. These traits all help to ensure that an indicator microorganism is detected in the environment in greater numbers than pathogens in every case.

5.4 Examples of Indicator Microorganisms

High concentrations of bacteria in the environment may indicate the presence of pathogens. For example, great numbers of bacteria in drinking water can signify that a nutrient of some sort has entered a distribution system or that disinfection has failed. However, total bacteria counts have many drawbacks as indicators because many factors can lead to high concentrations of bacteria in the environment other than contamination events. For example, non-pathogenic microorganisms are known to colonize drinking water distribution systems and increase total bacteria levels in water, but they may actually help to prevent exposure to pathogenic microorganisms by degrading them within the water distribution system.

Coliform bacteria, such as *E. coli*, are the most commonly used and well-studied indicator microorganisms. Coliform bacteria are normal inhabitants of the intestines of warm-blooded mammals and are more numerous than pathogenic bacteria in feces. The drinking water industry relies heavily on the detection on coliform bacteria to signal contamination of tap water. Coliform bacteria do not typically grow outside the body, so their presence in water suggests that it has been contaminated by feces. Water test kits are now available which have made the detection of coliform bacteria simple, cost-effective, and accurate. One commercially available kit tests for the presence or absence of coliforms in water. For this test, 100 mL of water is poured into a plastic bottle and sealed. If the water sample contains as few as one viable coliform bacterium, it will turn bright yellow within 24 hours. Using the same test kit, it is also possible to see if the coliform detected was *E. coli*. *E. coli* rarely grows outside of the body, so it is a more definitive, but less common indicator of fecal contamination than coliform bacteria. It should be noted, however, that there are many cases where *E. coli* have been detected in the absence of contamination (Rivera 1988).

Another group of bacteria present in feces may also signify that pathogens may be present in the environment. They are called *Enterococci* or fecal *Streptococci*. They are round, gram-positive bacteria which grow to high concentrations in the human digestive tract. There are some advantages to the use of *Enterococci* over coliforms as indicators of the presence of pathogens. Specifically, *Enterococci* rarely multiply in water, whereas this has been reported for coliforms. *Enterococci* also may be reliable indicators of disinfectant action, because they have been reported to be more resistant to disinfection than coliforms and they generally persist longer in the environment (Gleeson and Gray 1997).

Spore forming anaerobic bacteria, namely *Clostridia*, are microorganisms that may be indicative of past pollution and can be used as a tracer of less hardy indicators. They also can be used to indicate of the removal of parasites or viruses during drinking and wastewater treatment (Payment 1993). *Clostridia* remain in their environmentally resistant spore form in the presence of oxygen, which makes them a conservative indicator for pathogens that are not protected by spores. However, many anaerobic spore-forming bacteria are opportunistic pathogens themselves, and current test methods require a well-equipped laboratory to test for their presence.

Bacteriophages are viruses that only infect bacteria. They are useful indicator microorganisms because many of them, such as bacteriophage MS2, are nearly identical to human viruses in size, structure, and resistance to environmental stresses and disinfectants. There are two major types of bacteriophages, somatic and F-specific. To date, neither group has been agreed upon by microbiologists as the superior indicator species, but F-specific bacteriophages may be more indicative of contamination from human, rather than animal sources. By considering a bacteriophage's size, shape and hardiness, microbiologists can study environmental transmission of human viruses in a cost-effective and safe manner. These microorganisms are especially useful for describing viral transport to groundwater systems (Gerba 1984). Unfortunately, no clear link has been established between the concentration of bacteriophages and enteric viruses in sources of contamination. For this reason, they are most appropriately used as indicators of viral transport, rather than presence, in the environment. Bacteriophages provide a safe, useful way to study the behavior of human viruses.

Some new, non-viable indicators are helping microbiologists safely study the transport of bacteria and viruses in the environment. For example, novel, non-viable virus-like particles can be grown in the laboratory that are identical to viruses in terms of their outside appearance, but do not contain genetic material and thus cannot cause infection. Because they pose no risk of infection, these particles are a handy way to research the transport characteristics of human viruses in the environment. A similar concept is used to model the behavior of bacteria. For this, microbiologists use silicon-based fluorescent beads that are similar in size and shape to bacteria. The beads are inoculated into the environment and monitored without the risk of upsetting microbial ecology or causing disease. The beads also can be used in health care settings to assess the effectiveness of handwashing and cleaning procedures. Lotions containing high concentrations of these beads are now commercially available. To test the effectiveness of handwashing, the lotion is applied to hands and allowed to dry. Afterward, hands are washed, then illuminated with ultraviolet light. Providing a handy visual indication of the importance of thorough handwashing.

Many indicator microorganisms can be monitored at once to provide a complete picture of environmental contamination. For example, *Clostridium perfringens*, total and fecal coliform bacteria, and bacteriophages were used simultaneously to assess the risk of infection to communities near sewage sludge application sites (Brooks 2005). Levels of indicator microorganisms showed that land application of sewage sludge posed a negligible risk to communities from infectious agents transported through air, based on relationships between indicator microorganisms and pathogens.

5.5 Problems with Indicator Microorganisms

There are significant potential drawbacks associated with the use of indicator microorganisms. The most important drawback is that pathogenic microorganisms are sometimes present in the environment, even at high concentrations, in the absence of indicator microorganisms (Maier 2000). This is a major concern because it can result in transmission of infectious diseases without warning. This occurred in Milwaukee, Wisconsin, in 1993, when tests for fecal indicator microorganisms failed to show contamination of tap water while concentrations of the parasite *Cryptosporidium parvum* in water increased 100-fold. In part because the contamination of drinking water was not detected early, approximately 400,000 people became ill and approximately 100 died (MacKenzie 1994). Another drawback associated with indicator microorganisms is that they can be present in the absence of pathogens. Some indicator microorganisms can thrive in uncontaminated environments (Rivera 1988). This can result in false alarms and needless precautionary measures. For example, if levels of indicator bacteria in the water near Mission Beach in California exceed a certain threshold, authorities close the beach to prevent infections by pathogens. If indicators are present in the sample in the absence of pathogens, then the area experiences an unnecessary economic loss. Differences in survival and growth characteristics between indicators and pathogens can result in inaccurate assumptions about pathogen behavior. For example, microbiologists have learned a great deal about the action of disinfectants on pathogens by testing them on indicator microorganisms. This has allowed them to establish a general hierarchy of resistance to biocides for the different classes of microorganisms. However, the arrangement of the hierarchy can change for specific biocides and microorganisms. For example, *Cryptosporidium parvum* is highly resistant to chlorine, but is sensitive to ultraviolet light. In contrast, some viruses are resistant to ultraviolet light but are sensitive to chlorine. Another drawback of indicator microorganisms is that there are no reliable indicators available for some pathogens. For example, microbial indicators are poorly correlated with the presence of parasite cysts in water and there are no known indicator microorganisms for prions.

5.6 Chapter Summary

Microbiologists often predict the behavior and concentration of pathogens in the environment using indicator microorganisms. Many different microorganisms have been studied as indicators. Total bacteria are a useful indicator of pathogen concentration in drinking water. Coliform bacteria are the most commonly used indicator microorganisms and monitoring for their presence is required for drinking water and some other applications. *Enterococci* are useful indicators of fecal contamination, because they are excreted in great numbers in feces and do not routinely grow outside of the body. Spore-forming bacteria provide useful conservative indicators of contamination with pathogens because they are resistant to many environmental stresses and disinfectants. Bacteriophages are useful indicators of viral transport or transmission in the environment, but their correlation to the presence of viruses that infect humans in the environment is questionable. Particles resembling the size and shape of microorganisms may also be used to predict their behavior in the environment, particularly with respect to environmental transport. Unfortunately, the effectiveness of indicators may be hampered by physiological differences between indicators and pathogens that can affect their resistance profile to environmental stresses. As a result, there can be dangerous situations in which pathogens outnumber indicator microorganisms in the environment. For this reason, indicator microorganisms work best when used in combination with one another and validated by tests for pathogens.

Chapter 6

Infectious Disease Investigations

Synopsis

6.1 Chapter Preview

This chapter covers diagnostic microbiology and epidemiology, which are used to identify the source of infectious disease in an individual or in a disease outbreak. Diagnostic microbiological techniques enable scientists to compare microorganisms isolated from infections to microorganisms isolated from potential sources in the environment; if the microorganisms match, then the infection probably came from that source. Diagnostic microbiology is discussed first, beginning with specimen handling and processing, followed by conventional, immunological, and molecular test methods. Epidemiological investigations are also considered. Diagnostic microbiology and epidemiology are both important because investigation is a part of most infectious disease litigation and it requires a great deal of knowledge and expertise to be carried out correctly. This chapter will aid lawyers and judges who examine or create arguments based on diagnostic microbiology or epidemiology.

6.2 Introduction

Infectious disease investigations are carried out reasonably often in the United States. Some investigations focus on individual cases of disease while others center on disease outbreaks. Individuals are usually alerted to infectious disease transmission when their physician diagnoses them with an infectious disease. Public health agencies become aware of outbreaks through physician reports of disease channeled through infection control specialists at hospitals and through voluntary reports made by hospital laboratories and other channels, including the news media. Once a serious disease outbreak has been recognized, public health agencies may investigate it using diagnostic microbiology, epidemiology, or a combination of both techniques. However, only a small percentage of outbreaks are ultimately investigated. The Center for Disease Control and Prevention (CDC) investigates large or severe outbreaks in the United States. State and local public health agencies also investigate outbreaks but have fewer resources and normally work on smaller outbreaks occurring within defined regions. Public health authorities do not normally investigate individual cases of infectious disease unless the disease is very rare or has great potential for transmission to others. Investigations of individual infections are most often performed in support of litigation. Individual disease transmission events are typically investigated using diagnostic microbiology, because it is faster and because the individual usually suspects a particular source of infection.

Diagnostic microbiology is a powerful investigative tool. In its most simple form, it is used by physicians to identify the microbial cause of a disease in a patient or by industry to monitor the microbial quality of food or water. When diagnostic microbiology is used to investigate outbreaks, many specimens are collected and analyzed from both patients and potential sources of microorganisms in the environment. If a pathogen isolated from a potential source is shown to be identical to one isolated from a patient, then that source is likely to have caused the disease.

Diagnostic microbiology is extremely useful when samples are available for analysis and tests are performed properly. Unfortunately, samples are not always available and many factors can cause diagnostic microbiological tests to yield misleading results. For example, consider the diagnostic test for *Streptococcus pyogenes*, the bacterium that causes strep throat. For this test, a physician runs a sterile swab over the back a patient's throat and then submits the specimen to a laboratory for analysis, where laboratory workers rub the swab on blood agar plates. After incubation, bacteria that grow on the blood agar medium are compared to reference strains of *Streptococcus pyogenes* growing on the same medium. Incorrect results can arise from mistaking one patient's specimen for that of another, cross-contaminating the sample with a positive control specimen, or from defective growth media or environmental contamination. For this reason, specimen collection and handling procedures and microbiological tests must be performed competently by people who employ sufficient quality control measures.

Epidemiological methods are other investigative techniques that are used to identify the source of an infectious disease. Epidemiological investigations examine the distribution of disease in a population under the assumption that disease will be clustered in some way around the source. They are especially useful when there are no obvious sources to suspect, when diagnostic microbiology is too costly, or when specimens are not available for laboratory analysis. Epidemiological methods are also advantageous for less common scenarios, such as when the suspected agent of disease cannot be cultured in the laboratory or when it is unknown if disease is being caused by exposure to chemicals or microorganisms. However, epidemiological investigations are only as good as the data that are used to perform them and gathering unbiased information about the distribution of diseases in populations is challenging and time consuming.

Increases in travel and the centralization of food production are creating a trend toward disseminated, rather than clustered, outbreaks of disease in the United States. This makes outbreaks more difficult to detect because the number of infected individuals in any particular area may be low even though a great number of diseases may be occurring nationwide. Diagnostic investigations may not detect such outbreaks because there is very little communication between scientists isolating pathogens in different geographical regions. Epidemiological investigations of diffuse outbreaks are challenging because the majority of epidemiological investigations are carried out by state or local public health agencies and are geared toward detecting regional outbreaks. In addition, small public health offices rarely communicate the results of outbreak investigations at the national level. This means that there is a growing threat of outbreaks going undetected at the national level and underscores the importance of high standards of quality during infectious disease investigations.

6.3 False-Negative and False-Positive Results

False-negative results occur when microorganisms are present in a sample but are not detected by diagnostic tests. This can be caused by accidental destruction of microorganisms in specimens, use of inappropriate diagnostic tests, reagent failure, or microbiologist error. To avoid false-negative results, specimens should be refrigerated during transport and storage and tested as soon as possible after collection. Refrigeration is important because non-target microorganisms excrete toxic by-products during growth that can kill target microorganisms or obscure them during diagnostic testing. Freezing samples for storage should be avoided. Generally, the concentration of viable bacteria or viruses in a specimen will be reduced by 50 to 90 percent each time a specimen is frozen and thawed. Exposure of specimens to ultraviolet light also produces false-negative results. For example, fifteen minutes of exposure to sunlight can kill 90 percent of bacteria in a water sample (Fujioka 1982). Rapid changes in the saltiness, or ionic strength, of a specimen must be avoided because it causes microorganisms to burst and die. In addition, even very low concentrations of antimicrobial chemicals may kill microorganisms in specimens. This means that specimen transport containers should be dark, temperature controlled, contain an ionically balanced solution, and be free of antimicrobial chemicals including food preservatives. In addition, the appropriate test must be used to detect the type of microorganism in question. For example, fungal growth media should not be used for bacteria, because most fungal growth media contain antibiotics intended to inhibit the growth of bacteria in specimens. Finally, only fresh, sterile reagents should be used for microbiological analyses.

False-positive results occur when microorganisms are absent in a sample but are detected by diagnostic tests anyway. One source of false-positive results during diagnostic testing is cross-contamination. Cross-contamination occurs when a microbiologist accidentally transfers a target microorganism from a specimen that contains the microorganism to another specimen that does not contain the microorganism. For example, if a microbiologist were to obtain a specimen of ground beef from Manufacturer A using a small spoon, then take a sample from Manufacturer B without changing or sterilizing the spoon, then Manufacturer B's ground beef specimen could become cross-contaminated with microorganisms from Manufacturer A. Environmental contamination can also produce false-positive results, so appropriate precautions must be taken to ensure that specimens remain free of environmental or bodily microorganisms during testing. Microbiologists prevent environmental contamination by using aseptic techniques, which are procedures that reduce the likelihood that environmental microorganisms will contaminate a specimen. Aseptic techniques should always be used during sample collection and processing. Growth of target microorganisms in specimens should be avoided when determinations of microbial concentrations are being made from specimens to estimate exposure levels because it can result in artificial inflation of the perceived number of pathogens originally in the specimen. Typically, microbiological specimens are refrigerated at approximately 4°C and processed within forty-eight hours. However, certain microorganisms can grow at low temperatures, so the length of time between sample collection and processing should be minimized. This is particularly relevant to specimens taken from environmental sources, such as recreational water, food from restaurants and air from buildings because these specimens must often be transported to laboratories for analysis, which takes time.

Record-keeping errors can be as detrimental to the results of a test as environmental contamination or physical mishandling of specimens. A chain of custody record is one way to reduce the likelihood that errors in specimen handling or labeling will go undetected. A chain of custody record allows any scientist who handles a specimen to verify the length of time that the specimen was in their custody as well as the temperature of the specimen and the medium in which it was transported. Chain of custody forms are usually designed so that each handler retains a copy of the form upon giving the original to the next custodian, which makes mistakes easy to trace and correct.

6.4 Diagnostic Controls

Diagnostic controls help microbiologists detect false-negative and false-positive results and should be included during every type of diagnostic test. Many scientists include controls in their experimentation, but too few include thoughtful and appropriate experimental controls. Some microbiologists choose not to process control specimens to reduce labor or cost. Some microbiologists exclude control samples from tests because they feel that they are an insult to their ability or level of expertise.

Negative control specimens help microbiologists to recognize false-positive results. They are specimens that are known to be free of the pathogens of interest, but are identical to other specimens in every other way, including how the sample was collected, stored, and tested. Negative control samples should be processed both before and after the test samples. The first sample lets the microbiologist know if environmental contamination occurred during testing and the last sample indicates whether or not a reagent or other material became contaminated during testing. If a negative control sample gives a positive result, then the results of the test should be discarded and the test should be repeated if possible.

Positive control specimens help microbiologists recognize false-negative results. The positive control specimen should be a reference strain or clinically isolated microorganism that has been confirmed to be of a particular identity by an alternative identification method. Positive control samples should be run at the beginning of the test and again at the end if the assay is protracted or there is any chance of reagent failure. Positive control samples let microbiologists know that their tests are working and give them a reference to which they can compare other isolates if they appear to be positive for the target microorganism. If a positive or negative control does not produce the expected result, the attending microbiologist must not interpret the results of the test. Test results should be discarded and the test should be repeated if possible.

6.5 Good Laboratory Practices

Many diagnostic microbiologists recognize the potential for errors during testing and specify Standard Operating Procedures (SOPs) to prevent variability between tests and to serve as references for those who perform the test. SOPs are documents that provide detailed instructions on how to perform a particular task. Often, many SOPs are followed to complete one test. For example, if a laboratory employee wanted to isolate and identify *Pseudomonas aeruginosa* from a swimming pool, the employee may follow the SOPs entitled "Water collection for microbiological analysis," "Water sample storage," and "Detection of *Pseudomonas aeruginosa* in water." These SOPs would specify the instruments with which the water sample would be collected, environmental storage and transport conditions and other pertinent factors such as growth media and methods to confirm the identities of presumptive isolates of *Pseudomonas aeruginosa*. SOPs should be peer-reviewed and specify the author, edition, objective, materials needed, and procedure.

If a laboratory tests for microorganisms in accordance with scientifically valid SOPs and actively records and monitors the quality of testing, it is said to be following Good Laboratory Practice (GLP). GLPs are implemented to prevent laboratory errors, tampering with test results, and reduce the incidence of laboratory fraud. GLPs ensure that scientific tests are logical, transparent, and traceable.

Many laboratories are legally required to follow GLPs and it is appropriate for laboratories to follow GLPs voluntarily if their research will have a significant impact human health or the environment. Specific GLPs are required for microbiological tests submitted to the United States Food and Drug Association (FDA) and the United States Environmental Protection Agency (EPA). GLPs apply to chemical analyses, toxicological and microbiological tests. For example, if a company wishes to register an antimicrobial agent with the EPA so that it can claim that the product "disinfects" on the product label, the company must test its product for its ability to kill germs using EPA approved test methods under GLP conditions. To ensure that GLPs are followed, the USEPA and FDA have the legal authority to enter and inspect laboratories where products are tested. If government inspectors find evidence of scientific fraud or data manipulation, they have the authority to levy fines against offending laboratories and can immediately take action to remove inappropriately tested products from the marketplace.

6.6 Growth-Dependent Diagnostic Methods

Microbiologists frequently use a set of conventional, growth-dependent methods to isolate and identify pathogens from specimens. These procedures depend on isolating the microorganism from others in the specimen and then characterizing a pure culture of the microorganism using biochemical or microscopic analyses. The methods described below apply primarily to bacteria and fungi. Viruses are detected using expensive growth-dependent methods that assess their ability to infect mammalian cells grown artificially in the laboratory.

A first step in many growth-dependent diagnostic techniques is called selective enrichment. Selective enrichment is often necessary when the pathogen of concern is present in low numbers along with millions of other microorganisms, rendering it difficult to detect. To selectively enrich a sample, the microbiologist incubates the specimen in a growth medium which is specially designed to help the target microorganism outcompete environmental microorganisms, thus increasing the ratio of target to non-target microorganisms. After the sample has been selectively enriched, normal identification procedures can be used and it is likely that signs of the target microorganism, if present, will be observed.

The most important conventional tools that microbiologists use to isolate pure cultures of microorganisms from specimens are selective and differential media. Selective media are formulated according to the specific needs of certain types of microorganisms so that one type will grow while others are inhibited. For example, *Pseudomonas* bacteria can be isolated from a mixed culture by growing them on a medium that contains many different antibiotics. Since *Pseudomonas* bacteria are naturally resistant to a variety of antibiotics, they grow while other species do not. Microbiologists also use differential media to isolate pure cultures of microorganisms. Differential media allow many different types of microorganisms to grow but they cause those of interest to grow in a way that is distinct from of others. Color changes or other visual indicators normally accompany growth of target bacteria on differential media. For example, blood agar contains intact red blood cells (usually from a sheep) that are ruptured by growth by-products secreted by certain infectious agents, such as *Staphylococcus aureus*. Thus, when a mixed culture of bacteria is inoculated onto the plate and incubated, *Staphylococcus aureus* colonies can be differentiated from others by the halo of blood cell destruction that appears around those bacterial colonies. Some microbial growth media are both differential and selective. For example, m-ENDO medium is differential and selective for coliforms. When an environmental sample containing coliforms and other bacteria is inoculated onto m-ENDO, coliforms grow as greenish-gold colonies while other bacteria are inhibited. A variety of selective and differential media are available for the many groups and species of microorganisms.

Once a microorganism has been isolated from a sample and a pure culture has been obtained, microbiologists confirm the identity of the isolate by performing a series of biochemical analyses and microscopic observation. Biochemical analyses differentiate bacteria by assessing their ability to react with certain chemicals or degrade certain food sources (See Table 6.1). For example, one of the defining characteristics of enteric bacteria is their ability to ferment lactose a sugar that many other bacteria cannot degrade. Microbiologists can confirm the identity of an isolate by assessing its biochemical profile. There are even rapid tests available that allow microbiologists to test a wide range of metabolic capabilities all at once. Another way to confirm the identity of an isolate is to observe it with a microscope. This is most informative after individual colonies of microorganisms have been isolated. Gram-stains are a reliable reference and provide information about the basic morphology of the isolated bacterium. Staining procedures also can be used to assess whether microorganisms in a specimen are alive or dead.

Table 6.1
Important Metabolic Indicators for Bacteria

Type of Bacterium	Important Metabolic Indicator
Enteric bacteria	Fermentation of various carbohydrates
Salmonella	Hydrogen sulfide production
E. coli	Indole production
Klebsiella, Enterobacter	Citrate utilization
Staphylococcus	Catalase enzyme
Staphylococcus	Coagulase enzyme

One of the major drawbacks to conventional microbiological methods is that they cannot detect viable but non-culturable microorganisms, which are microorganisms that microbiologists have not yet been able to grow in the laboratory. For example, microbiologists have not yet determined how to grow noroviruses in culture, but they are a leading cause of foodborne illness. Other microorganisms can be grown, but the methods involved are cost or time prohibitive. Some examples of microorganisms that are not practically culturable in a clinical setting include bacteria that cause syphilis, *Chlamydia*, and tuberculosis. To illustrate how some of these tests are impractical, consider that the bacterium that causes syphilis can only be grown in the footpad of the nine-banded armadillo. Viable but non-culturable microorganisms may present health risks, but these pathogens cannot be detected using conventional methods.

6.7 Molecular Diagnostic Methods

Current molecular methods for pathogen detection are based on the polymerase chain reaction (PCR). PCR was developed in 1985 and has revolutionized the way pathogens are detected and characterized in clinical specimens and the environment. During a PCR, a specific segment of DNA is replicated repeatedly through a series of reaction cycles. Each cycle of the PCR doubles the amount of target DNA in the sample; one strand becomes two, two strands become four, and so on. After millions of identical strands have been formed, the DNA can be visualized in the laboratory. RNA primers are a key part of the PCR reaction because they stick to specific sequences on the DNA strand and tell the reactive enzymes where to start and stop copying DNA. This means that by carefully choosing which RNA primers are used, microbiologists can test specimens for DNA that is specific to one particular subspecies of pathogen, DNA from a group of pathogens, or DNA associated with toxins. If the DNA in question gets replicated during PCR, then the microbiologist knows that the pathogen or toxin was present in the specimen. If no DNA is amplified, then the microbiologist concludes that the microorganism of interest was not present in the sample.

PCR is useful because it detects genetic material rather than microbial growth. This means that PCR can be used to detect non-culturable microorganisms such as noroviruses. PCR is commonly used by microbiologists to detect pathogens in the environment. For example, norovirus (stomach flu) outbreaks aboard cruise ships are detected and confirmed using PCR. One major benefit of PCR is that it reduces the amount of time needed to get the results of a microbiological test because the scientist doesn't have to wait for the microorganisms to grow. A relatively new technology, called real-time PCR, has cut detection times to between 1 and 3 hours, in contrast to conventional detection times that range between one and fourteen days. This technology is very valuable in circumstances where detection time is critical. For example, mechanical "spore-sniffers" based on real-time PCR were used extensively by government agencies to detect anthrax in mail distribution centers after the anthrax attacks of 2001. One of the most attractive qualities of PCR is that it enables a microbiologist to look for the genes that encode particular toxins produced by bacteria and fungi, rather than the microorganisms themselves. One theory is that microbiologists will eventually assess the hazard associated with a clinical or environmental specimen by the ability of the microorganisms within the specimen to produce relevant toxins, rather than by the number or species of bacteria present in the sample (which may or may not carry genes required for toxin production).

One molecular diagnostic technique that is very relevant to infectious disease litigation is pulsed-field gel electrophoresis (PFGE). During PFGE, enzymes are used to cut DNA from a bacterial isolate into small pieces, which are then separated according to their size by electricity in a gel-like matrix. PFGE is used to "fingerprint" bacterial pathogens based on their genetic makeup, in much the same way that DNA from human specimens is fingerprinted. By comparing the DNA fingerprint generated by PFGE from one bacterium to that of another, a microbiologist can assess the likelihood that they came from the same source. Matched PFGE fingerprints are the most definitive way to show that a clinically isolated bacterium originated from a particular source in the environment.

The major drawback of molecular methods is that they do not provide microbiologists with information about the viability of the microorganism detected. Because PCR detects DNA and DNA is relatively stable in the environment even after a microorganism has died, a positive PCR result does not necessarily indicate that there is a risk to health. For example, a PCR may indicate that enteric viruses are present in drinking water after chlorination, but the likelihood that the DNA detected was part of an intact and functional virus is low. Another drawback of PCR is that it requires a great degree of knowledge to carry out successfully. In addition, a greater chance of sample contamination exists than for conventional techniques because DNA is resistant in the environment and extraordinary amounts of DNA from past PCRs can contaminate surfaces and liquids in laboratories.

6.8 Immunological Diagnostic Methods

Immunological methods are useful to microbiologists. Immunological methods are based on antibodies produced by mammals, which bind strongly to specific pathogens. The two major uses of this technology during infectious disease investigations are to confirm that a patient was exposed to a microorganism at some time in the past and to provide detailed, strain-specific information about the identity of a pathogen cultured from a clinical specimen.

Antibodies are the foundation of immunological methods. Our bodies come equipped with a suite of various antibodies that are designed not to react with human tissues but to bind strongly to foreign material, including microorganisms. During the first years of life, many of our antibodies are received through breast milk, which contains high concentrations of antibodies specific to many different pathogens. Once the immune system becomes self-sufficient, the body manufactures a broad range of antibodies. During infections, the body learns to secrete antibodies specifically targeting the foreign material. If the infection is chronic or severe, the specificity of antibodies produced against the pathogen increases. After a few infections or one major infection with a microorganism, antibodies develop that bind very strongly to the outer surface of the infectious agent.

One way in which microbiologists use antibodies is by adding antibodies specific to a particular pathogen (usually collected from the blood of serially exposed rabbits) to a specimen and observing antibody binding. In basic tests, binding is signaled by coagulation within the specimen. However, microbiologists can also detect antibody-pathogen binding by using specially engineered antibodies that emit light when bound to a target. If light emission is observed, then the microbiologist knows that a specific microorganism is present in the sample.

Microbiologists also can use antibodies to indicate if a person was exposed to a pathogen at some time in the past. To do this, microbiologists simply observe whether or not an antibody against a particular pathogen is present in a clinical specimen. If a pathogen-specific antibody is detected, then the microbiologist knows that exposure has occurred, because the immune system has produced antibodies to fight the infection. This is the basis of many modern clinical tests for pathogens and diseases, including modern tests for HIV, which take less than thirty minutes.

The most common and versatile immunological test method is called the Enzyme Linked Immuno-Sorbent Assay (ELISA). In an ELISA, either known antibodies or known antigens are coated onto the bottom of a plastic dish. Specimen is added and depending on the type of ELISA, either antibodies or antigens bind to the specimen. After this step, a second antibody is added, which fluoresces when in contact with antibody-antigen complex, allowing the extent of specific antibody-antigen interactions to be quantified using light detecting instruments. ELISAs are useful because they make it possible to test many specimens at once for antibodies against a particular pathogen or to test one specimen for antibodies against many different pathogens.

6.9 Epidemiological Investigations

The power of epidemiology was first demonstrated in 1849, when John Snow performed his famous and pioneering investigation of a cholera outbreak in London. During the outbreak, he carefully plotted on a map the geographical distribution of disease, then compared that to the locations of street pumps used for drinking water. He observed that most cholera cases were clustered around a single pump located on Broad Street. Suspecting that it was the source of disease, he removed the handle. Within days, the number of deaths from cholera dropped significantly and the outbreak subsided. Through his investigation and action, the Broad Street pump was determined to be the main source of the outbreak, many lives were saved, and epidemiology was born.

The basic premise of epidemiology is that disease does not occur randomly but rather in discernible patterns that reflect the underlying cause of the disease (Friis 1999). Epidemiological investigations involve establishing a case definition, assessing the characteristics of the population that contains cases and analyzing the distribution of cases within the population. A number of experimental designs are available for epidemiological disease investigations, but the method most commonly used for infections disease outbreak investigations is called a case-control study. In a case-control study, two groups are designated from within a population, one in which everyone has the disease of interest, and one in which everyone is free of the disease. Case control studies attempt to determine the way in which the two groups differ, under the assumption that the difference will indicate the cause of the disease. For example, consider a population of people who attend a hypothetical summer picnic, where of twenty people in attendance, ten fall ill soon afterwards with diarrhea. The epidemiological investigation would begin by defining the population. Depending on a number of factors, the population could include all people outdoors in that location on that particular day, all people outdoors in that location for that week, the group of people attending the picnic, or some other group. A good population to start with would be those who attended the picnic. To investigate, the population could be broken into two groups of ten, those who became ill and those who remained healthy. Surveys could then be taken from all in attendance to assess broadly the various exposures to potential sources of disease throughout the day. Potential sources could be the food eaten, physical contact with a particular person, or ingestion of water from a particular source. If, when the results are tallied, a high percentage of the people who became ill all also ate the potato salad and those who remained healthy did not, then the study would indicate the potato salad as a very likely source of the outbreak.

In practice, epidemiological investigations do not always demonstrate such clear relationships between sources of exposure and disease outcome. Thus, it is crucial to ensure that epidemiological studies have a strong statistical foundation and that all possible sources of error are taken into account before conclusions are drawn. Considerations include, among other things, relevant vaccinations, use of antibiotics, and the status of the immune system. In addition, case definitions that are too broad or narrow can cause study error. Ultimately, the study director determines the level of statistical rigor required to draw conclusions. Epidemiologists typically report correlations only if statistics show that there is less than a 5 percent chance that the correlation came about by chance. In other words, epidemiological conclusions are normally considered valid if they are at or above the 95 percent confidence level. If they are below this level of confidence, then the study is considered to be inconclusive.

The results of neutral health department epidemiological investigations usually carry much more weight in the courtroom than testimony from paid expert witnesses (Marler 2005). In addition, many epidemiological studies can be validated in some way. For example, John Snow's investigation of cholera was validated by the reduction of disease in the area after the handle of the Broad Street water pump was removed and disease subsided. Currently, a sample of material from the suspected source can be analyzed for the suspected microorganism to validate conclusions. This is accepted practice whenever samples are available for analysis.

6.10 Chapter Summary

Diagnostic microbiology is used to isolate, identify or confirm the presence of an infectious agent in a clinical specimen or in the environment and can be used to link a disease to a suspected source. Sample collection and handling must be performed with great care to avoid sample contamination, which can occur from environmental microorganisms or cross-contamination of specimens. In addition, samples for microbial analysis must be handled carefully so that microorganisms do not grow or are not inadvertently destroyed by environmental factors such as ultraviolet light. Many laboratories voluntarily follow Good Laboratory Practices (GLPs) through a series of approved Standard Operating Procedures (SOPs) to combat variability. Some laboratories are required to have extensive quality control measures in place to satisfy regulatory agencies such as the FDA and EPA. There are three basic ways in which microbiologists isolate and identify microorganisms from the environment. Conventional methods involve growth of microorganisms on selective or differential media, but many microorganisms are not easily grown in the laboratory. Immunological methods, including ELISA assays, are a useful means to identify microorganisms or check to see if someone has experienced an infection in the past. Immunological methods are commonly used in clinical settings. Molecular methods, primarily based on PCR, rapidly detect genetic material and can detect non-culturable infectious agents, but do not indicate whether or not the microorganism was alive when it was collected. Positive and negative control specimens should always be included in all diagnostic tests, and any aberrant results in these controls indicate complete failure of the test with respect to all samples. When diagnostic microbiology cannot be used because samples are not available or because there are no suspected sources of disease, epidemiological methods can identify the source of an infectious disease outbreak. The basic premise of analytic epidemiology is that disease does not occur randomly but rather in discernible patterns that reflect the underlying cause of the disease. The case-control study is the most common type of study for infectious disease investigations. In practice, the correlation between exposure to a potential source and disease should be at or above the 95 percent confidence level to be considered valid.

Chapter 7

Waterborne Microbial Diseases

Synopsis

7.1 Chapter Preview

This chapter describes waterborne diseases in terms of their prevalence, causes, and consequences, focusing on those that circulate in the United States. Both those caused by drinking water and those caused by recreational water are discussed. In addition, sources of water contamination are identified. This chapter takes a holistic view of waterborne disease prevention, emphasizing not only the final act of disinfecting drinking and swimming pool water, but also effective wastewater treatment as a means to keep the load of waterborne pathogens low in the environment. Drinking water and wastewater treatment processes are outlined with a focus on the relevance of each treatment step to pathogen removal from water. Finally, pathogens that are commonly implicated in waterborne disease transmission are discussed one-by-one, focusing on the physiological characteristics that enable their transmission through water and examples of outbreaks they have caused.

7.2 Introduction

Infections from water have afflicted mankind since recorded history, ranging in severity from nuisances to killers. Polio, cholera, typhoid fever, and hepatitis A are dreadful waterborne diseases that are prevalent in many parts of the world. In developed countries, many deadly waterborne diseases have been eradicated through aggressive vaccination programs and thorough drinking water and wastewater treatment programs. Water in the United States is the safest it has ever been but painful and incapacitating waterborne infections and outbreaks still occur. Familiar contemporary waterborne microorganisms include hardy hepatitis A virus, noroviruses, the disinfectant resistant parasites *Cryptosporidium* and *Giardia*, and the toxin-producing strains of *E. coli* and *Shigella* bacteria. In addition virulent waterborne microorganisms still circulate in other countries and are frequently reintroduced to the United States by travelers and migrant laborers. To ensure that waterborne outbreaks do not occur, water must be treated vigilantly.

The true prevalence of waterborne disease in the United States remains a mystery because diseases are frequently unreported by individuals and because waterborne microorganisms may be difficult or costly to detect in clinical specimens. Approximately twenty-five outbreaks of waterborne disease are reported each year in the United States. However, outbreak reports only come from communities with active disease surveillance programs and only include outbreaks that are deemed important enough to investigate. Most municipalities have no requirement for reporting outbreaks. Thus, the true prevalence of waterborne disease in the United States is probably much higher than that which is reported.

Ingestion or physical contact with microbially contaminated drinking, recreational, or bathing water causes waterborne diseases. Most pathogens transmitted by water infect the intestines and cause diarrhea. Most of the time, these pathogens are spread by ingestion of contaminated drinking water. Since people in the same area usually share a source of drinking water, diseases from drinking water tend to occur as localized rather than diffuse outbreaks. Recreational water is also a source of waterborne diseases. Diseases from recreational water are usually caused by ingestion of water but can also be caused by skin contact. For example, the bacterium *Pseudomonas aeruginosa*, which is common in many aquatic environments, can cause folliculitis, or irritation of the skin, in individuals who use spas.

Waterborne disease litigation can be challenging because a great number of legal theories may be employed against water contaminators, because litigation may involve the question of sovereign immunity for water providers and because class-action lawsuits are frequently warranted. In addition, the true source of waterborne disease outbreaks may be difficult or costly to pinpoint during discovery. Fortunately, water treatment facilities are required to maintain extensive records of treatment process variables and to perform regular water microbiology tests.

7.3 Water Contamination

Wastewater (sewage) is replete with pathogens and is a major source of microbiological water contamination. Cities produce enormous volumes of wastewater each day. Most wastewater is treated to reduce levels of pathogens by centralized wastewater treatment plants, but a significant percentage is treated by decentralized systems including septic tanks. After treatment, a large amount of wastewater eventually goes to bodies of fresh water that are used as sources of drinking water. For septic tanks, treated wastewater either evaporates or leaches deep into the ground. Municipal wastewater treatment plants usually dispense their treated wastewater into to some receiving body of water. In some cases, entire bodies of water consist solely of treated wastewater. For example, the city of Tucson, Arizona, drains effluent into a channel formed by the Santa Rita River. Upstream from the wastewater outflow, the river channel is dry for most of the year. Downstream, it is a lush, perennial river replete with waterfowl and vegetation. Unfortunately, even treated wastewater can contain appreciable levels of pathogens. Thus, many outbreaks of waterborne disease are eventually traced to contamination of water by wastewater. Since wastewater treatment facilities are designed to remove a consistent fraction of, but not all, pathogens, treated wastewater provides water bodies with a constant influx of pathogens. The harsh properties of the environment help to reduce pathogen concentrations in surface water, but some pathogens survive nonetheless. One interesting study highlighted the potential for contamination of water from sewage. In the study, scientists purposefully added a harmless tracer virus (a bacteriophage) to toilets in homes on the Florida Keys. They were able to detect the tracer virus in the nearby ocean within just hours, underscoring the importance of wastewater as a source of pathogens in water.

Animal waste is another major source of water contamination. Domestic animals are the predominant source, although there have been a few cases where waterborne diseases have been traced to wild animals such as beavers and waterfowl. Unlike human waste, which almost always undergoes some type of treatment before being released to water, animal wastes are minimally treated, if treated at all, before being released into the environment. This can result in high concentrations of pathogens entering water because the intestines of grazers are frequently colonized with high levels of pathogens, such as *E. coli* O157:H7 and *Cryptosporidium parvum*. Centralized meat production facilities, also known as concentrated feeding operations, and dairies release large volumes of minimally treated animal waste into the environment.

All of the sources of water contamination added together can produce a low-level "background" contamination of water reservoirs, otherwise known as a pathogen burden. At this point, scientists do not fully understand the impact of low-level pathogen burdens on human health. However, low-level contamination can be amplified under certain circumstances. For example, oysters, which are filter feeders, tend to concentrate waterborne pathogens in their tissues and are a known source of many waterborne disease agents including noroviruses and hepatitis A virus. In one study, oysters were collected from thirty-six U.S. bays from the West, East, and Gulf coasts. When analyzed, 7.4 percent of all oysters collected contained *Salmonella* (Brands 2005). Low-level contamination of water bodies is probably not a major concern if water is disinfected prior to consumption, but it may have a significant impact on infectious disease transmission under certain circumstances, such as when it is concentrated by shellfish.

7.4 Drinking Water and Disease

Most waterborne diseases come from contaminated drinking water. In fact, around 94 percent of waterborne disease outbreaks have been caused by contaminated drinking water with each outbreak affecting, on average, 495 victims (Craun 1999). More outbreaks of waterborne disease have been caused by contaminated groundwater than by contaminated lakes or streams and most outbreaks are associated with decentralized water sources like rural wells. Two factors lead to infections from wells. First, water from wells is not always treated with disinfectants, meaning that contaminants that enter aquifers may pass unhindered to the tap. Second, most rural homes rely on septic systems for sewage treatment, which are notorious sources of waterborne pathogens. Septic systems are large underground collection tanks that reduce the number of pathogens in wastewater by natural attenuation of pathogens during extended storage. In a properly functioning septic system, wastewater is treated for a few weeks. It then trickles into the ground containing low levels of pathogens. Unfortunately, septic systems are notoriously leaky and neglected, resulting in untreated, highly contaminated wastewater leaching freely into the ground. Pathogens can then travel through soil to nearby aquifers, causing waterborne disease.

Centralized sources of drinking water can also spread waterborne pathogens. Unlike rural wells, which provide drinking water to a few or a few hundred people, drinking water from centralized water treatment facilities can cause hundreds of thousands of cases of disease if contamination arises. For example, in 1993, water serving the city of Milwaukee, Wisconsin, became contaminated with the waterborne parasite *Cryptosporidium parvum*, originally from infected cattle. During an outbreak lasting approximately two weeks, 400,000 people became infected and around 100 people died as a result of the infection (MacKenzie 1994; Hoxie 1996). The magnitude of this outbreak highlights the importance of robust water disinfection procedures at large water treatment facilities to prevent waterborne disease outbreaks.

Water can become contaminated with pathogens at the source or during distribution, but contamination may be difficult to detect using standard microbiological procedures. Drinking water should be treated to kill pathogens prior to bottling or distribution through pipes. Most drinking water utilities maintain a low concentration of disinfectant in the water after treatment to protect consumers from contamination during distribution. Chlorine and chloramines are the most common disinfectants for drinking water, but chlorine dioxide, bromine, ozone, and ultraviolet light may also be used. Municipal utilities provide most of the drinking water in the United States. They must meet certain microbiological criteria to ensure that their product is safe (less than 1 coliform per 100 mL of water).

7.5 Recreational Water and Disease

Waterborne diseases are regularly transmitted through recreation in lakes, streams, swimming pools, and spas. Recent research suggests that of investigated recreational outbreaks, 15 percent are caused by *Cryptosporidium,* 14 percent are caused by *Pseudomonas,* 13 percent are caused by *Shigella,* 11 percent are caused by *Naegleria*, 6 percent are caused by *Giardia*, and 6 percent are caused by toxigenic *E. coli.* In 23 percent of outbreaks, no causative microorganism is identified (Craun 2005). Waterborne pathogens that demonstrate transmission through recreational water are usually marked by their ability to withstand harsh environments, by excretion from infected people in great numbers, and by low infectious doses. Simple hygienic precautions, such as keeping infants out of swimming pools and sufficiently treating wastewater discharged to recreational lakes and streams, helps reduce levels of pathogens in recreational water bodies. Disinfectant chemicals and water filters can be used as a barrier to recreational waterborne disease transmission in swimming pools and spas but cannot be used in natural waters because of the adverse impact on the environment and cost.

Many different waterborne pathogens are transmitted in inadequately disinfected swimming pools. These pathogens include a variety of bacteria, parasites, and viruses. Bacteria transmitted through poorly maintained pools can include *Salmonella*, *Shigella*, *E. coli*, and *Pseudomonas*. Poliovirus, norovirus, hepatitis A virus, and rotavirus also have the potential for transmission through swimming pools. The protozoan parasites *Giardia and Cryptosporidium* are major problems in swimming pools. The parasite *Cryptosporidium parvum*, for example, is especially resistant to chlorine and has been the source of many disease outbreaks in swimming pools (See Table 7.1) (Tanner 2005). Fortunately, these parasites are relatively large and can be trapped by well-maintained pool filters.

Table 7.1
Selected Outbreaks of *Cryptosporidium* from Swimming Pools

Year and Locale	Symptoms	Number Infected	Disinfection	Special Circumstances
1988, California	Diarrhea and Fever	60	Adequate chlorine level	Two cases were hospitalized and 32 sought physician consultation
1988, U.K.	Diarrhea	79	Not specified	Onset of illness occurred after swimming in children's pool
1990, Vancouver, B.C.	Fatigue, nausea, weight loss, diarrhea	87	Chlorine residual below minimum recommended level of 0.5 mg/L	The children's pool remained closed for 10 days for cleaning
1992, Oregon	Diarrhea, vomiting, fever	55	Not specified	Outbreak subsided after the pool water was drained and replaced
1993, Wisconsin	Diarrhea	62	Not specified	Possible connection to the large drinking-water based outbreak in Milwaukee
1997-1998, Australia	Diarrhea, vomiting	52	Adequate chlorine level	Pools were treated with chlorine dioxide to inactivate oocysts
2000, Ohio	Diarrhea	700	Not specified	93.6% of patients reported swimming in a single pool
2000, Nebraska	Diarrhea	225	Not specified	Many patients reported swimming while they were ill, which may have prolonged the outbreak

Spas are another recreational body of water linked to recreational waterborne disease transmission. (Table 7.2) Water in spas is hot enough to kill most of the pathogens relevant to swimming pools over time. However, the waterborne bacterium *Legionella pneumophila* can produce severe disease and is able to grow at high temperatures in improperly disinfected whirlpools, hot tubs and spas. When inhaled, *Legionella* causes a pneumonia-like illness called Legionnaires' disease and a similar, flu-like disease called Pontiac fever. Legionnaires' disease largely affects people fifty years old or older, with 50 percent of hospitalized cases resulting in mortality. Pontiac fever is a much milder form of *Legionella* infection, in which all infected individuals recover. Interestingly, *Legionella* may be protected from chemical disinfectants in spas by being able to grow inside larger microorganisms called protozoa. Protozoa are able to form cysts under adverse conditions, which may help the *Legionella* survive disinfection. In one study, *Legionella* contained in protozoan cysts were protected from at least 50 mg/L free chlorine (Kilvington 1990). Many cases of Legionellosis acquired from contaminated whirlpools and hot tubs have been described in scientific literature (Tanner 2005).

7.6 Wastewater Treatment

Wastewater treatment is crucial to keeping water clean and safe. As a result, wastewater treatment facilities are part of nearly every community. Today, more than 15,000 wastewater treatment plants treat more than 150 billion gallons of wastewater per day in the United States alone (Maier 2000). Without wastewater treatment, the nutrients in the waste people produce each day would quickly overwhelm our environment. Furthermore, wastewater contains around a million pathogens per gallon. Thus, a large city like New York churns out trillions and trillions of pathogens per day. If released directly into the environment, those pathogens would contaminate drinking water, resulting in widespread disease.

Table 7.2
Selected Outbreaks of *Legionella* from Recreational Spas

Year and Locale	Symptoms	Number Infected	Disinfection	Special Circumstances
1981, Vermont	Legionnaires' Disease	34	No detectable free chlorine	pH was maintained at 7.4
1985, Michigan	Legionnaires' Disease	14	4 to 6 ppm bromine	Nearby air conditioner tested positive for *Legionella*
1992, Colorado	Legionnaires' Disease	13	Not specified	PCR showed that *Legionella* was in the water
1998, Wisconsin	Legionnaires' Disease	45	17 ppm bromine	Whirlpool was well-brominated
1996, Virginia	Pontiac Fever	2	None performed	Whirlpool served as a display model at a flower show and was not intended for use
1994, Aboard a cruise ship	Pontiac Fever	50	Not specified	Protracted outbreak occurred between April 30, 1994 and July 9, 1994
1999, Georgia	Pontiac Fever, Legionnaires' Disease	2	2 ppm bromine	Legionnaires' Disease and Pontiac fever were transmitted by the same source
1987, Vermont	Pontiac Fever	3	Not specified	*Legionella* recovered directly from whirlpool water

Modern wastewater treatment consists of three major steps, each of which plays a part in reducing the number of pathogens in wastewater. (Figure 7.1) First, water is treated physically in a process known as primary treatment. During this stage, wastewater is passed through a bar screen and grit chamber. Then it is sent to a large tank where heavier particles settle to the bottom and smaller ones remain in solution. Scum on the top and particles on the bottom of the tank are collected and sent to anaerobic tanks for digestion. Together, they are known as sewage sludge. After treatment, sewage sludge can be applied to land as "biosolids," a reasonably safe fertilizer that contains fewer pathogens. Water in the middle of the settling tank eventually flows on to the second stage of treatment, known as secondary or biological treatment. During secondary treatment, the trillions of microorganisms in wastewater are metabolically activated to digest contaminants (including pathogens) and remove organic material from the water. To activate the microorganisms, water is passed through an aeration tank, which provides ample oxygen for degrading small bits of organic material. Wastewater can also be passed over a trickling filter, where water slowly trickles over the filter matrix giving resident microorganisms on the filter a chance to bind to and degrade contaminants in the water. Sometimes, wastewater undergoes tertiary treatment. During this step, physical or chemical means can be used to remove or kill the bulk of remaining pathogens. Most commonly, it is passed through a large sand or mixed media filter to trap any remaining pathogens, especially environmentally resistant parasitic cysts. It is then chlorinated and de-chlorinated, and released to the environment.

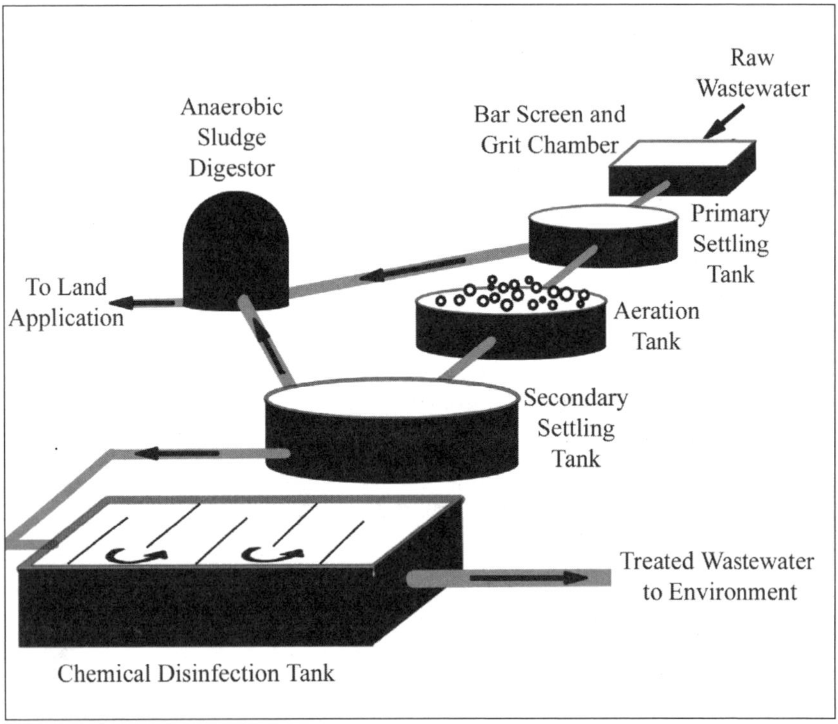

Figure 7.1 *Diagram of a wastewater treatment process.*

Wastewater treatment plant effluent is required by the Clean Water Act to contain fewer than 200 fecal coliforms per 100 mL of water. In some cases, more stringent limits on pathogen content may be imposed. Wastewater treatment systems are not foolproof, and many factors can adversely affect facility performance. When treatment plants fail, billions of pathogens may be released to the environment, leading to concentrated pulses of pathogens entering surface water. If allowed to occur, transitory pulses of pathogens entering the environment tend to amplify the cycle of waterborne disease transmission. Many times, wastewater treatment plants are affected by events beyond the control of plant operators. During heavy rain, for example, plant operators may be forced to reduce water residence times to avoid back-flooding of raw wastewater. Reduced water residence time in the facility compromises the microbial quality of effluent by reducing the amount of treatment the water receives. Wastewater treatment plants may also be adversely affected by changes in chemical properties of the influent water that decrease the metabolic activity of the beneficial microorganisms that remove pathogens and other organic matter during treatment. Power outages can also adversely affect wastewater treatment plants. For example, when power grids on the East Coast failed during August of 2003, billions of gallons of raw wastewater flowed into the Great Lakes, which are relied on as a source of drinking water. The quality of treated wastewater can also be adversely affected by human error. For example, insufficient concentrations of disinfectant chemicals may be added during physiochemical treatment. Additionally, wastewater treatment plant infrastructure, such as trickling filter beds, must be maintained properly using special techniques to ensure that biological degradation of wastewater remains efficient.

Treated wastewater is ultimately pumped into nearby bodies of water for disposal, used for irrigation, or applied to land in order to recharge underground aquifers. In most cases, wastewater treatment plant effluent is simply pumped into a lake, stream, or the ocean. Occasionally, it is released to wetlands, providing time for natural environmental processes to further reduce levels of pathogens and other organic contaminants. Wastewater is sometimes used to irrigate crops because it may provide beneficial fertilizing chemicals, such as nitrogen.

7.7 Drinking Water Treatment

Many waterborne disease outbreaks are caused by a breakdown in the potable water treatment process that allows pathogens to travel from raw water (groundwater, lake or stream water) to the tap without sufficient exposure to disinfectant chemicals. Therefore, adequate treatment of drinking water is essential to protect the public from waterborne disease outbreaks. Drinking water treatment is required under the law for most public systems. The USEPA requires through the Safe Drinking Water Act that drinking water contain no detectable coliforms (indicator bacteria) per 100 milliliters.

Conventional drinking water treatment consists of preliminary disinfection, coagulation, flocculation, sedimentation, filtration, and final disinfection. (Figure 7.2) However, some steps may not be necessary if high-quality source water is used, such as pristine groundwater. If source water is murky or contains organic matter, it must be first treated physically to remove particulates so that disinfectants will kill microorganisms effectively. Conventional drinking water treatment is described here, assuming poor to normal source water quality. In the first step, water from a source such as a lake or stream is chlorinated to reduce the number of pathogens entering the treatment system. Next, coagulant chemicals are added to the water, which cause suspended organic matter to form large clumps during stirring. This stirring is known as flocculation. After water is flocculated, the clumps are removed allowing them to settle in basins or be trapped in high-volume filters. Taken together, the physical treatment processes of coagulation, flocculation, sedimentation, and filtration remove approximately 99 percent of microbial contaminants from source water (Maier 2000). Physical treatments are especially crucial for removing parasites in the form of cysts, because cysts are resistant to chlorination but can be removed by filtration. After filtration, water is disinfected by oxidant chemicals such as ozone gas, chlorine, and chloramines, or by ultraviolet light. Chlorine is the most common disinfectant used for drinking water disinfection.

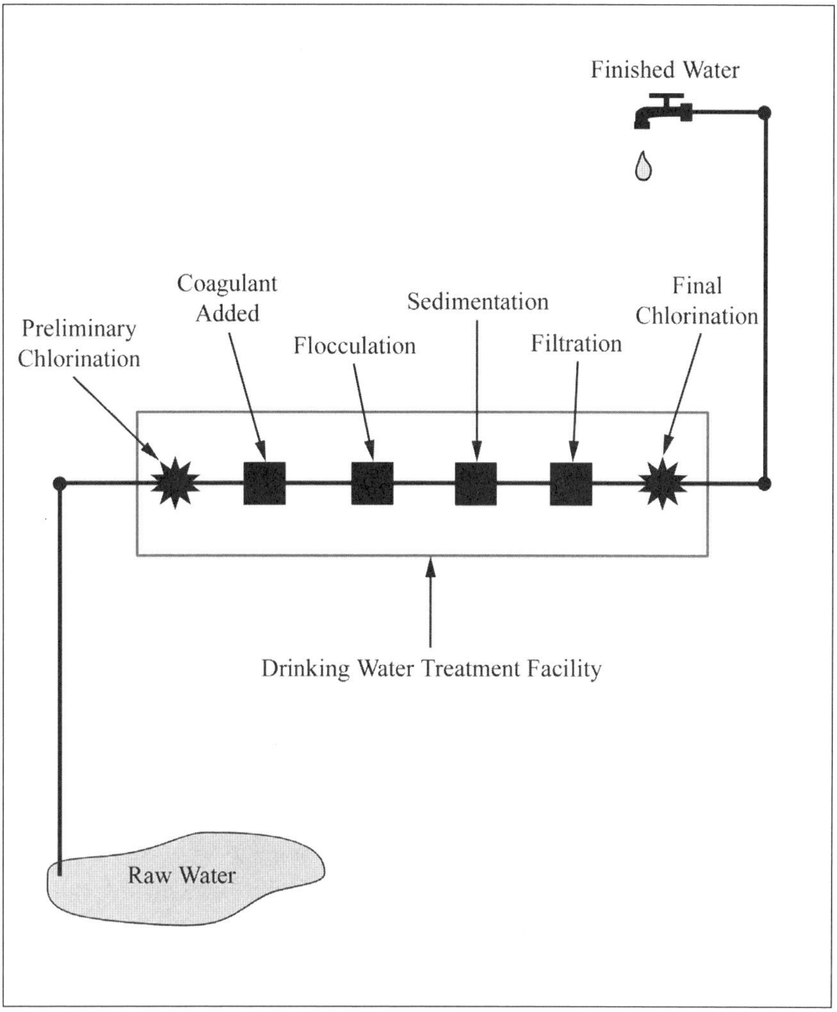

Figure 7.2 *Diagram of a drinking water treatment process.*

Certain factors interfere with drinking water disinfectants. With oxidant chemicals such as chlorine, chloramines, chorine dioxide, and ozone, the most important factor is the amount of organic matter present in the water. These chemicals destroy microorganisms by oxidizing them. However, the chemicals cannot distinguish organic matter in the form of bacteria from other organics. Thus, organic materials in drinking water compete with microorganisms for oxidation. In practice, this means that dirty water (even if not visually dirty) requires much more disinfectant to kill the same number of bacteria. In addition, water temperature can affect the activity of disinfectants. When temperatures are lower, chemical reactions progress more slowly, meaning that disinfectants work more slowly as well. One obvious exception to this rule is ultraviolet light, which is not a chemical and functions the same regardless of water temperature. The amount of organic material in the water, temperature, and the nature of microbial contaminants all influence the efficacy of chemical disinfectants.

A small amount of disinfectant residual left in water serves as a fail-safe to prevent bacterial growth and to kill pathogens in the event of an intrusion into the distribution system. Chlorine is safe enough to be consumed in small quantities and many water utilities intentionally maintain a chlorine residual of around 0.2 parts per million during water distribution (LeChevallier 1999). One particular source of contamination during water distribution highlights the importance of disinfectant residuals. Temporary reverses in water pressure occur as a result of routine occurrences during water distribution through pipes, such as when a large drinking water pump is shut off temporarily for servicing or when a lightning strike prevents electricity from reaching a pump. During these times, known as temporary pressure transients, raw sewage from leaky sewage pipes running below and parallel to drinking water lines can literally be sucked into the drinking water lines. When pressure is reinstated, pathogens from the sewage can be delivered directly to the tap (LeChevallier 2003). Because most drinking water contains small amounts of chlorine, events such as these do not necessarily result in waterborne disease.

In order to control pathogens, disinfectant concentrations must be maintained for sufficient lengths of time. However, some disinfectants are more potent than others. Thus, water microbiologists often describe disinfectants using the *Ct* concept, where *C* is the disinfectant concentration and *t* the time required to inactivate a certain percentage of microorganisms in water at a certain temperature. The multiplication of the two values produces a number that allows for comparison of disinfectant effectiveness in general and with respect to different microbes or water conditions. The *Ct* concept, when applied to drinking or recreational water, helps professionals in the field determine the amount of disinfectant needed to kill pathogens during water treatment. The *Ct* concept can also be used to assess the amount of disinfectant needed to handle isolated contamination events. For example, if a warm swimming pool became contaminated with the parasite *Giardia lamblia*, a chlorine concentration of twenty parts per million (ten times the normal disinfectant level) would need to be maintained for more than twenty-three minutes to inactivate 99.9 percent of the cysts, according to the published *Ct* value of sixty-eight for *Giardia* (Tanner 2004).

7.8 Commonly Implicated Pathogens

Shigella

Shigella are gram-negative, rod shaped bacteria that can colonize the human intestine and are pathogenic. Four species of *Shigella* are linked to disease in humans, including *Shigella dysenteriae, sonnei, boydii,* and *flexneri*. *Shigella* are excreted in the feces of infected humans and are marked by their high infectivity (infectious dose of only around 200 organisms) and by the ability to produce a potent enterotoxin called shiga-toxin. Infections with this microorganism usually involve profuse, often bloody, diarrhea. In certain susceptible individuals including children, infection can cause deadly hemolytic-uremic-syndrome (HUS), intestinal bleeding, and other severe symptoms. HUS is caused by the action of shiga-toxin on the kidneys and individuals afflicted with HUS may lose the use of their kidneys completely.

Animals are not a reservoir for *Shigella*. Thus, most cases of shigellosis result from either direct (person-to-person) or indirect transmission of the bacteria. Shigellosis is commonly spread through water and food handling. *Shigella* can survive in cool water for days, but is not considered to be environmentally hardy. This bacterium is sensitive to standard disinfectants used to treat drinking water. Outbreaks of shigellosis appear to be declining in the United States, probably as a result of more consistent wastewater and drinking water treatment procedures. Because this microorganism is also transmissible through person-to-person contact via the fecal-oral route and is very infectious, shigellosis initially acquired from water may spread to family members or colleagues in a phenomenon known as called secondary disease transmission.

Enterotoxigenic Escherichia coli (E. coli)

Enterotoxigenic *Escherichia coli* are gram-negative, rod-shaped bacteria characterized by residence in the intestines of warm-blooded animals and the ability to ferment lactose at elevated temperatures. They are known to reproduce both in the presence and absence of oxygen. Enterotoxigenic *E. coli* are different than enterohemorrhagic *E. coli* (including *E. coli* O157:H7), but both bacteria produce a potent intestinal toxin that causes profuse diarrhea. Unlike enterohemorrhagic *E. coli* O157:H7, (usually spread by food), enterotoxigenic *E. coli* infections are rarely fatal and do not result in kidney damage. Enterotoxigenic *E. coli* is the common cause of "traveler's diarrhea." Although this pathogen is not prevalent in drinking water in the United States, many travelers take infections home from abroad. As a result occasional infections from recreational water can be traced to this type of *E. coli*.

Pseudomonas aeruginosa

Pseudomonas aeruginosa is a gram-negative, rod-shaped bacterium that is ubiquitous in the environment. It can be a source of waterborne infections. It is generally very hardy, and its ability to spread through water is enhanced by special characteristics. First, *Pseudomonas aeruginosa* can grow quickly to great numbers in water if disinfectants are not present even if nutrients are scarce. Second, *Pseudomonas aeruginosa* is more resistant to disinfectants than many other waterborne bacteria because it produces a slimy coat.

The primary symptom of waterborne infections from *Pseudomonas aeruginosa* are ear infections and irritation of the skin, but infection may also result in respiratory infections if susceptible individuals inhale small droplets containing the bacteria. Waterborne transmission of this pathogen is of particular concern to those afflicted with cystic fibrosis, because *Pseudomonas aeruginosa* can colonize and obstruct the airway. Interestingly, *Pseudomonas aeruginosa* can also contaminate contact lens cleaning solutions, leading to eye infections. Treatment of *Pseudomonas* infections can be difficult because it is resistant to many antibiotics and is known to acquire resistance genes from other species of bacteria.

Vibrio cholerae

The microorganism that causes cholera, *Vibrio cholerae*, is a gram-negative, rod-shaped bacterium. Unlike other bacteria, which may be spread in many ways, *Vibrio cholerae* is almost always transmitted through water. *Vibrio cholerae* secretes a potent enterotoxin called Cholera A-B toxin. This toxin causes the intestines to reverse the direction in which electrolytes and water are pumped, resulting in diarrhea so profuse that death may come within two days without treatment. *Vibrio cholerae* is a problem in many tropical areas, although it is not prevalent in the United States.

Cholera is the quintessential waterborne disease and has a long history of pandemics. Scientists now believe that this microorganism establishes a symbiosis with marine algae, allowing it to travel great distances to initiate pandemics when conditions are appropriate for its transmission (Epstein 1993). Cholera kills many people worldwide, mostly children. Since the last cholera pandemic in 1991, scientists estimate that there have been 1 million cases and 10,000 deaths (Brock 2000). Interestingly, cholera is almost never lethal in developed countries. Treatment of cholera is very simple and does not require drugs. Instead, the fluid and electrolytes lost in diarrhea are replaced through oral or intravenous fluids. Doctors simply measure the volume of fluid lost and ensure that the same volume of salty fluid is replaced. Eventually, the body clears the infection. Death from cholera in developing countries occurs primarily because people do not have access to sufficient amounts of clean water and do not know that electrolytes must be replaced along with lost water.

Cryptosporidium parvum

Cryptosporidium parvum is a protozoan parasite that is excreted in the feces of infected humans and many wild and domesticated mammals. *Cryptosporidium* forms oocysts, which are resistant to chemical disinfectants. As an oocyt, *Cryptosporidium* is very stable and may survive for weeks in natural waters such as rivers and lakes at cool temperatures. However, as temperatures increase, *Cryptosporidium* oocysts are inactivated at a faster rate. Millions of oocysts are usually present in one gram of feces from an infected person. Studies with human volunteers have shown that only one to a few organisms must be ingested to initiate infection (DuPont et al. 1995). Many infected people become asymptomatic carriers (people who show no symptoms of infection, but still excrete *Cryptosporidium* in their feces).

Cryptosporidium has caused numerous waterborne outbreaks in North America and Europe. This parasite commonly infects young children and the immunocompromised, affecting between 2 and 5 percent of people each year in developed countries. In 1993, it caused the largest waterborne disease outbreak ever documented in the United States (MacKenzie 1994). In healthy people it causes an infection lasting from seven to ten days. However, it can be a life threatening illness in immunocompromised individuals, including people with acquired immunodeficiency syndrome (AIDS), the very young, and people undergoing certain treatments for cancer. There is currently no treatment available for *Cryptosporidium* infection.

Giardia lamblia

Giardia lamblia is a waterborne protozoan parasite that is commonly harbored in the intestines of wild and domesticated animals. Like *Cryptosporidium parvum*, *Giardia lamblia* is shed in feces in the form of an environmentally resistant cyst. Cysts remain dormant in the environment until ingested by a warm-blooded animal. After ingestion, stomach acids trigger the parasite to excyst, where it travels to the small intestine and attaches itself to the intestinal wall using disks that resemble suction cups. Infections with *Giardia lamblia* are characterized by persistent, foul-smelling diarrhea. Disease normally lasts from one to four weeks, during which millions of cysts are shed in feces. Giardiasis can be treated with the drug metronidazole. If left untreated, infections may persist for months.

Giardia lamblia has been associated with infections from both drinking and recreational water. Common sources of the parasite in the environment are warm-blooded animals that harbor the parasite in their intestines. Beavers and muskrats are especially significant; one study estimated that infected beavers shed one hundred million *Giardia* cysts per day (Hibler 1990). In one outbreak from drinking water, people were infected with *Giardia lamblia* in Vail, Colorado. Ultimately, researchers traced the infections to the wild beavers that lived in the stream that provided the town's drinking water.

Naegleria fowleri

Naegleria fowleri is a naturally occurring, free-living amoeba that can cause waterborne disease. This pathogen is known to infect children by entering nasal passages and sinuses along with water during recreation. After entering nasal passages, the amoeba breed and spread, causing swelling and destruction of the brain. Infections progress rapidly, usually causing disease within twenty-four to fourty-eight hours of exposure. Because of the fast pace with which the infection progresses and because of difficulties with diagnosis, infections are almost always fatal. *Naegleria* do not usually infect adults.

Naegleria infections are highly associated with swimming in lakes and streams, but have also been documented as a result of contaminated bathtub water (Marciano-Cabral 2003). Infections from potable water can be prevented by disinfection. Unfortunately, the only way to prevent infections from contaminated lakes and streams is avoid swimming in these waters. Scientists are just beginning to learn about the prevalence and ecology of these deadly amoebas.

7.9 Chapter Summary

Contaminated drinking and recreational water spreads waterborne diseases. Water is most frequently contaminated by fecal material from humans or domestic animals and is occasionally contaminated by pathogens from wild animals or aquatic sediments. Prevention of waterborne diseases depends on keeping the numbers of pathogens circulating in the environment low and on thoroughly and consistently disinfecting swimming pool water and drinking water. Wastewater treatment is a remarkably effective means of reducing pathogen numbers in water, and does so through physical removal, biological degradation, and chemical disinfection. If treated in accordance with the law, wastewater contains fewer that 200 fecal coliforms per 100 mL. Drinking water treatment facilities create potable water through a process that consists of preliminary disinfection, coagulation, flocculation, sedimentation, filtration, and final disinfection. Although drinking water treatment facilities deliver safe water most of the time, large influxes of pathogens into treatment facilities and poor source water quality can result in treatment failure and severe outbreaks of disease. Six pathogens are commonly associated with waterborne diseases in the United States. They include the disinfectant-resistant parasites *Giardia lamblia* and *Cryptosporidium parvum*, specific strains of the bacteria *Shigella*, *E. coli*, and *Pseudomonas*, and the free-living amoeba *Naegleria fowleri*.

Chapter 8

Foodborne Microbial Diseases

Synopsis

8.1 Chapter Preview

Food is an important medium of disease transmission and foodborne diseases are frequently litigated. This chapter explores some features common to foodborne diseases and strategies for legal claim substantiation. Because foodborne disease outbreaks often originate during agriculture or raw food processing and storage, this chapter describes a mechanism by which food safety can be assured throughout food production. Proper food service and handling is also discussed as a way to prevent foodborne disease outbreaks. Some common foodborne microorganisms are presented with descriptions of likely sources of pathogens in food and instances of foodborne disease outbreaks. By reading this chapter, lawyers and judges will gain a better understanding of the microorganisms that cause foodborne disease outbreaks, how to substantiate disease claims in court and the particular features of the microorganisms that cause foodborne outbreaks.

8.2 Introduction

Although food in the developed world is safer to eat now than ever before, contaminated food remains a major source of infectious disease. This is partially due to the countless ways in which food can become contaminated with disease-causing microorganisms. Contamination of food may occur at the food source, during food processing, packaging, handling, preparation, or storage. Today, food destined for consumption in one country may be produced and packaged in another country half a world away. In many countries, sanitation is poor and outbreaks of disease occur frequently among food workers. Compounding these problems with contamination, food commonly undergoes lengthy transport, which can allow infectious microorganisms to grow. As a result, microorganisms have been isolated from nearly every food, from *E. coli* O157:H7 in apple cider to *Salmonella* in sausage. Unfortunately, the vast majority of foodborne disease outbreaks are not reported to physicians and public health agencies.

There are two main types of foodborne disease, intoxication from foodborne toxins and infection from foodborne microorganisms. Both types of disease are frequently referred to as food poisoning. In a case of classical food intoxication, enterotoxins produced by bacteria in food are ingested and cause disease when they contact the gastrointestinal tract. No microorganisms need actually be ingested, and the time before the onset of disease ranges from one to twenty-four hours. The archetypal foodborne intoxication stems from potato salad consumed at a picnic throughout a hot day. *Staphylococcus aureus* bacteria, originally from the cook's hand, grow and produce toxins in the potato salad. The first few people who eat the salad don't become ill, but as the day progresses, the dose of bacterial enterotoxins increases with each serving. Attendees of the picnic later realize that everyone who ate the potato salad late in the day was stricken with nausea, diarrhea, and vomiting. Foodborne intoxication is probably a minor source of foodborne disease relative to foodborne infections. During a foodborne infection, the pathogen multiplies within the gastrointestinal tract and may concurrently produce toxins to produce disease. The length of time before disease sets in can range from days to weeks.

Ingestion of virulent foodborne pathogens can result in debilitating and life-threatening infections. For example, the bacterium *E. coli* O157:H7 can produce complete and permanent kidney damage. Ingestion of certain bacterial toxins, such as botulinum toxin from improperly canned food, can cause paralysis and death. Parasites found in contaminated meats can damage the muscles, lungs and brain. In addition to the insult of infection from food, many foodborne pathogens are capable of secondary disease transmission, meaning that they spread from an infected individual to others via alternative routes of infection, such as water or surfaces. Thus, an infected family member may put their family at risk of infection from a foodborne pathogen, even if the family does not consume any contaminated food.

Recent foodborne disease outbreaks have resulted in some highly visible litigation. In the late 1990s, consumption of contaminated, undercooked hamburger at a fast food restaurant led to a number of infections with highly virulent *E. coli* O157:H7. Ensuing litigation was later settled out of court for more than one million dollars per infected person, and for more than fifteen million dollars for a young girl who suffered permanent kidney damage. More recently, a foodborne disease outbreak spread from green onions contaminated with hepatitis A virus at a Mexican Food restaurant chain. This outbreak resulted in hundreds of infections, deaths, and significant litigation.

Consumers are entitled to a reasonable certainty that their food, as ingested, will be free from disease-causing microorganisms. Although an acceptable risk of foodborne infection has yet to be established, it is reasonable to believe that it should be less than or equal to the commonly accepted risk for infection from ingestion of drinking water of fewer than one infection per 10,000 people per year. To this end, many food-manufacturing facilities integrate tests for microbial contaminants into the food-making process under Good Manufacturing Practices (GMP) and Hazard Analysis and Critical Control Points (HACCP), discussed later.

8.3 Pathogens in the Food Supply

Bacteria, viruses, and parasites that live in the intestines of cattle, swine, and poultry are the predominant source of pathogens in meat. Many of these microorganisms are harmless to the animal but have the ability to cause disease in humans. For example, a small percentage of cattle can be expected to harbor great numbers of the virulent human parasite *Cryptosporidium parvum* in their intestines with few, if any, signs of illness. During butchering and meat processing, it is not uncommon for meat to become contaminated with intestinal microorganisms. The potential for this type of contamination exists for all meat animals. In beef, *E. coli* O157:H7 is a major concern. In poultry, *Salmonella* and

Campylobacter have proven to be problematic. A variety of microorganisms may cause contamination of pork, and parasites that can infect humans are also a significant contaminant.

Contamination of fruits and vegetables with pathogenic microorganisms is a concern during farming. Irrigation water often comes to crops from untreated bodies of water such as lakes and streams, and may contain high levels of disease-causing microorganisms. In some countries, wastewater may be used to irrigate food crops. Interestingly, microorganisms contained in the contaminated water are rarely found inside of fruits or vegetables. Edible surfaces, however, are easily contaminated by unsanitary irrigation water. Scientists have shown that even low concentrations of certain types of microorganisms in irrigation water can contaminate lettuce and other foods and bring about significant risks of infection. These findings are particularly relevant to contaminants that can cause infection at low doses and that are resistant to environmental degradation (Stine 2005).

Fruits and vegetables are usually rinsed prior to shipment or storage to remove dirt, lower microbial concentrations, and increase freshness. However, great amounts of produce may pass through the same rinse water before being sold to consumers. This means that if contamination of the rinse water occurs, many people may become infected. To properly rinse and decontaminate produce, levels of disinfectant chemicals in the water must be properly and adequately maintained with an appropriate dosing system. This is especially important if the rinse water becomes dirty, because the ability of disinfectants to kill microorganisms is drastically reduced in the presence of organic matter (Tanner 2004). To ensure the safety of produce rinse water, disinfectant levels should be confirmed from time to time with inexpensive instruments such as chlorine test strips. For foods eaten raw or slightly cooked, inadequate rinsing procedures may actually enhance the spread of foodborne illness by spreading the microorganisms from one seriously contaminated batch to other, previously uncontaminated, batches.

8.4 Contamination During Food Processing and Service

Although the majority of food processing plants and restaurants produce and serve safe food, poor sanitation and cost cutting measures increase the risk of foodborne disease. Most food processing environments are well-funded, efficient and generally safe work environments. In cases where the plant workforce is generally frenzied, ignorant, or lazy, the potential for foodborne disease outbreaks increases greatly. Restaurants, too, may be hectic places to work. In the quest for profit, restaurant managers may neglect to teach food handlers how to prevent foodborne disease outbreaks. In both food processing plants and restaurants, common but negligent behaviors precipitate foodborne disease outbreaks.

Improperly thawed foods contribute to the growth of foodborne disease agents in both food processing and food service. During extended thawing, temperatures can be reached that allow microorganisms to grow and multiply food. This increases the chance of disease transmission if food is not cooked thoroughly. This is especially hazardous for uncooked foods like sushi. The length of time foods, especially meats, remain at room temperature prior to cooking should be limited. This type of contamination probably led to severe outbreaks of *E. coli* O157:H7 at fast food restaurants serving hamburgers in the late 1990s.

Meats and vegetables should be marinated with great care to reduce the likelihood that microorganisms will grow, because marinades usually include all of the nutrients necessary for bacteria to reproduce. Marination should always be performed in a refrigerator and marinated foods should be kept at refrigerated temperatures for no more than one day. Used marinades should be assumed to contain high levels of bacteria and should not be poured on cooked foods or re-used for other raw ingredients. Even in a highly contaminated marinade, there are not always aesthetic indications that pathogenic microorganisms are present.

Cross-contaminated food is undoubtedly a major source of foodborne illness, but outbreaks from this type of contamination may be difficult to trace. Cross-contamination most frequently occurs when a microbially contaminated food, which is intended to be cooked, comes into contact with a food that is intended to be eaten raw. Cross contamination should be suspected when a disease agent is isolated from a food in which it is not normally found. For example, if *E. coli* O157:H7 were detected in lettuce at a fast food restaurant, it would not be unreasonable to suspect that the original source of the contagion was contaminated hamburger, given that hamburger is the most common source of *E. coli* O157:H7.

One of the most effective ways to ensure that food products do not leave the manufacturing plant containing contaminants is to include a post-processing pasteurization step before canning or bottling. During pasteurization, foods are heated to a high temperature for a short period of time. While not sufficient to kill all bacteria, pasteurization is remarkably effective for killing pathogens in food. Many modern foods are pasteurized, including orange juice, milk, and eggs.

Canning of foods has been practiced for hundreds of years as a way to preserve foods for long periods of time. In general, canned foods are microbiologically safer than foods packaged in other manners because can contents are heated and oxygen is removed from the can, which kills most microorganisms and inhibits most others from growing in the can. Ironically, the canning process itself may cause outbreaks of foodborne disease. Contamination of canned foods can occur from leaky can seams, insufficient heating of can contents, or spoiled contents before packaging. One microorganism in particular, *Clostridium botulinum*, is an important disease agent in canned foods (discussed below).

8.5 The HACCP System for Assuring Food Safety

The Hazard Analysis and Critical Control Point (HACCP) system is a proactive, systematic, and widely accepted way to assure food safety during manufacturing. The key characteristic of HACCP is the analysis of raw materials for microbial contamination, without heavy reliance on final product testing. Under HACCP, one assumes that if no major sources of contamination are missed, and manufacturing processes such as pasteurization are confirmed to be effective, then the final food product will be safe. Further information regarding this system can be found in Sperber (1991), and Simonsen, *et al.* (1987). Before HACCP can be implemented, a generally hygienic and stable food preparation or processing environment is required. In other words, the food processing plant should use Good Manufacturing Practices (GMP). Further information about GMP can be found in Moberg (1989).

If HACCP is used during food manufacturing, seven tasks must be performed. First, the establishment will attempt to assess the hazards and risks associated with all aspects of the food being manufactured, from growing and harvesting to preparation and consumption. Next, the establishment will identify the Critical Control Points (CCP) necessary to control those hazards. For each of these hazards, the establishment will determine the critical limits that are appropriate. The establishment will stipulate how CCP monitoring is to be performed. Importantly, the establishment will specify corrective procedures to be taken in the event that a CCP limit is reached. The establishment will also verify that the HACCP system is working properly. Lastly, the establishment will implement accurate and thorough record keeping procedures to document the HACCP plan (Jay 2000).

In the spirit of HACCP, foodborne disease prevention can begin as early as the design phase for some commercially produced foods. For example, if a company were to develop a salad dressing, ingredients could be chosen not only by availability, cost, and contribution to taste, but also by their potential for microbial contamination. If possible, ingredients with a high potential for microbial contamination, such as raw eggs, could be excluded from the formula to enhance the safety of the food product. Additionally, pH, saltiness, and oil content could be adjusted against the nutritional requirements of the likely foodborne contaminants in the raw ingredients of the salad dressing to enhance the safety of the product.

If HACCP is used diligently and appropriately during food manufacturing, outbreaks of disease from food should be very rare. In the case that a food product from a HACCP-conforming facility were to cause disease, it will probably be difficult to show negligence on the behalf of the food producer. However, if HACCP is used incorrectly or without full commitment to food safety, it may result in a false sense of protection from foodborne disease.

8.6 Substantiation of Foodborne Disease Claims

Foodborne disease outbreaks are revealed in a number of ways. If one or a few individuals acquire a foodborne disease, claims are likely to be self-reported to doctors and sometimes directly to lawyers. The claimant will usually have a suspicion of which meal was responsible along with some kind of justification, such as a meal having an "off" taste or odor. If many individuals acquire a foodborne disease, the outbreak may be reported to local public health and surveillance agencies that get information through reports from physicians and hospital infection control practitioners.

Foodborne disease claims are best substantiated by the results from diagnostic microbiology or epidemiology, but the opinion of expert witnesses can also be important. Local public health agencies rely heavily on epidemiological methods to determine the source of a disease outbreak.

Epidemiological investigations take a great deal of time but they can be effective if enough data is available and they are done properly. The results of neutral health department investigations usually carry much more weight in the courtroom than testimony from paid expert witnesses (Marler 2005). If an epidemiological evaluation of the disease outbreak was not conducted, the link between a particular food and disease can still be established in court using diagnostic microbiology, expert testimony, or a combination of both. Without question, the most effective way to prove that a disease came from a particular source is to isolate the same microorganism from both a clinical specimen and from the suspected source. It may even be possible to show that the two microorganisms are identical by genetic fingerprinting. If both sources cannot be tested, for example if the suspected source of the pathogen was thrown away or the causative microorganism was never isolated during medical treatment, then other options are available. For example, a physician's description of disease symptoms may be sufficient to show that disease was caused by a specific pathogen. One can also build an argument that a particular food or restaurant was the most likely source of a specific infection based on characteristic incubation periods of foodborne infections and the association of the causative microorganism with particular foods present in the restaurant. In addition, health department records may be obtained to gauge the hygiene and practices of the suspected food-handling establishment. If it can be shown that an establishment consistently mishandles or prepares a suspected food, in addition to having a poor hygiene record, the claim may hold up in court.

8.7 Commonly Implicated Pathogens

Salmonella and *Campylobacter*

Although they differ in terms of their genetics and shape, *Salmonella* and *Campylobacter* have many things in common with respect to foodborne disease. This is because both bacteria reside in large numbers in the intestinal tracts of poultry. To a lesser extent, both bacteria also inhabit the intestines of other warm-blooded livestock. As a result, both *Salmonella* and *Campylobacter* are most commonly associated with food poisoning from undercooked poultry. Both bacteria cause self-limiting but potentially severe diarrhea in humans. Both are stabilized by refrigeration and easily killed by cooking.

There are over a thousand strains of *Salmonella*, all of which are thought to be able to cause illness. *Salmonella* are gram-negative, rod-shaped bacteria that produce disease by colonizing the intestines and invading intestinal cells. *Salmonella* also produce potent enterotoxins, which result in diarrhea. The cause of typhoid fever, *Salmonella typhi*, is a unique and particularly virulent foodborne pathogen that is prevalent in developing countries and is associated with a high rate of mortality. Foodborne outbreaks of typhoid fever in the United States are rare.

Although similar in many respects, *Campylobacter* is different from *Salmonella* because far fewer species are known to cause disease and it is less tolerant to the presence of oxygen. Like *Salmonella*, *Campylobacter* are highly associated with contaminated or undercooked poultry. The most notorious species are *Campylobacter jejuni*, and *Campylobacter fetus*, which together account for a large percentage of foodborne illness among children. It should be noted, however, that many *Campylobacter* infections have been traced to infected pets, including dogs.

Staphylococcus aureus

Staphylococcus are gram-positive, round bacteria which are notably resistant to being dried on a surface. *Staphylococcus aureus* is the species most commonly associated with foodborne disease, although others are sometimes noted.

Staphylococcus aureus colonizes nearly every warm-blooded animal, including humans, and may be found in many foods as a result of contamination during food handling or processing. It normally inhabits bodily openings such as the nostrils and thousands may live on a square centimeter of skin. *Staphylococcus aureus* produces toxins optimally at temperatures just above that of the human body. It is also highly tolerant of salts, which makes it particularly relevant to some food products in terms of its ability to thrive. *Staphylococcus aureus* is a unique agent of foodborne disease because symptoms are usually associated with ingestion of preformed toxins in food, rather than with colonization of the bacteria in the gut. Disease from food poisoning by *Staphylococcus aureus* is very rarely associated with mortality. Usually, a person ingests a small amount of toxin (less than 30 nanograms of toxin has been shown to produce disease in humans) and falls ill between one and six hours later. Symptoms of *Sta-*

phylococcus food poisoning include vomiting, severe diarrhea, and nausea. There are no treatments for Staphylococcal intoxication.

Listeria monocytogenes

Listeria monocytogenes is a gram positive, rod-shaped bacterium that is tolerant to acids, salts, and low temperatures. It is commonly found in raw milk, cheeses, poultry, and other fresh and frozen meats. Unlike most other microorganisms, *Listeria monocytogenes* is capable of growth during refrigeration. For this reason, unpasteurized milk products or ready-to-eat meats kept at low temperatures can be sources of *Listeria monocytogenes*. To help prevent the growth of this bacterium, meat and dairy products should be pasteurized or stored frozen whenever possible.

Infection with *Listeria monocytogenes* is called listeriosis. If ingested in sufficient quantities, *Listeria monocytogenes* invades the cells of the intestinal wall and sometimes spreads to the bloodstream, causing sepsis and meningitis. Although many people are probably exposed to these bacteria in food, only a small fraction of people fall ill. Those who develop listeriosis are usually immunocompromised as a result of AIDS, chemotherapy, or age. Fetuses can also become infected. Once an individual is infected, listeriosis results in death in approximately 25 percent of clinical cases.

Clostridia

Clostridia are spore forming, anaerobic, gram-positive, rod-shaped bacteria that are known for their ability to produce potent toxins and resist environmental degradation. *Clostridium difficile, Clostridium perfringens*, and *Clostridium botulinum* are sources of foodborne illness in raw meat and canned foods and are common inhabitants of the intestines of warm-blooded animals. While growing in food, *Clostridium* is no more resistant to stress than other bacteria. In the environment, however, *Clostridium* is most often found as a spore, making it resistant to heat, ultraviolet light, dessication, and many common disinfectants.

Although they are members of the same genus, different foodborne species of *Clostridia* produce distinct types of foodborne diseases. *Clostridium perfringens* and *Clostridium difficile* causes disease by producing enterotoxins that cause diarrhea and intestinal cramps. Alternatively, *Clostridium botulinum* causes botulism, a very serious disease in which bacterial toxins (the same toxins used in BoTox treatments) are consumed in contaminated food and gradually paralyze the body. If intoxication is severe, the muscles of the heart and lungs can become paralyzed, leading to death. *Clostridium botulinum* is particularly dangerous in the anaerobic environment of canned foods where it can grow and secrete toxins without indication of spoilage. Heat is effective for controlling this microorganism during the canning process and many outbreaks have been traced to improper canning procedures. In addition, raw honey is a source of botulism. During honey making, bees can concentrate *Clostridium botulinum* in honey. This disease most often occurs in infants, where the bacteria sporulate and grow in the intestines, producing toxins and causing paralysis. Adults are afforded some protection from the disease by fully established intestinal microflora and by experienced immune systems.

Escherichia coli (E. coli)

Escherichia coli are gram-negative, rod-shaped bacteria characterized by residence in the intestines of warm-blooded animals and the ability to ferment lactose at elevated temperatures. They are known to reproduce both in the presence and absence of oxygen. Interestingly, the vast majority of *E. coli* strains are not associated with disease, and may even play a beneficial role in digestion of food in the intestines.

E. coli is one of the most notorious and publicly recognized pathogens. Four subgroups of *E. coli* are recognized causes of foodborne disease. These subgroups include enteroaggregative, enteropathogenic, enterotoxigenic, and enterohemorrhagic *E. coli*. Enteroaggregative *E. coli* is characterized by its ability to adhere tightly to and colonize the intestinal wall. It secretes enterotoxins, which can produce diarrhea. Enteropathogenic *E. coli* is known to invade the cells of the intestinal wall, eliciting a severe immune response in the host and causing diarrhea. Enterotoxigenic *E. coli* is the common cause of traveler's diarrhea and is most prevalent in water, although it can also be spread by food. It secretes a host of enterotoxins, which result in profuse, watery diarrhea, vomiting and nausea. The last group, enterohemorrhagic *E. coli*, causes intestinal bleeding and produces the potent *stx* enterotoxin, which can cause permanent kidney damage in severe cases. Although most people are susceptible to infection by enterohemorrhagic *E. coli*, children and the elderly most often experience kidney damage caused by Hemolytic Uremic Syndrome (HUS). One member of this group, *E. coli* O157:H7, has been responsible for a number of severe foodborne disease outbreaks associated with contaminated hamburger. In addition to hamburger, enterohemorrhagic *E. coli* have caused outbreaks through alfalfa sprouts, cake, coleslaw, apple cider, and raw milk. Mortality rates from foodborne enterohemorrhagic *E. coli* outbreaks have been documented above 20 percent, and regularly range from 1 to 5 percent.

Norovirus

Noroviruses are small, round, structured viruses belonging to the family *Caliciviridae*. Norwalk virus is the most notorious norovirus. Noroviruses cannot currently be grown in the laboratory. Instead, they can be detected in stool samples using electron microscopy or in the environment using molecular methods. Because technologies for the detection of noroviruses are developing, outbreaks caused by these viruses frequently go undetected or are unconfirmed. At this point, the true incidence of norovirus infection remains unknown. Interestingly, previous infection with noroviruses provides no defense against new infections with the virus.

Noroviruses are a major cause of foodborne disease (Gerba 2003). Norovirus infection is characterized by profuse, sudden onset of diarrhea and forceful vomiting. Humans and cattle are thought to be the only reservoirs of this virus, and contamination of food most likely occurs when feces contaminate food, either directly or indirectly. Some of the largest outbreaks of this virus have occurred on cruise ships as a result of contaminated food. In some cases, outbreaks were so severe that hundreds of people were stricken and vessels were forced to return to port. In most cases decontamination of environmental surfaces and food was effective in preventing outbreaks on subsequent voyages. There is currently no treatment available for norovirus infection.

Hepatitis A virus

Hepatitis A virus is a small, round virus that utilizes RNA as its genetic material. Hepatitis A virus is a member of the family *Picornaviridae*. When ingested, the virus infects cells in the intestines and then is ultimately transmitted to cells in the liver. While in the liver, hepatitis A virus multiplies rapidly, often resulting in a brief, or acute, loss of liver function. Infection is characterized by an incubation period of between fifteen and forty-five days, followed by jaundice for a period of approximately two weeks. During incubation, the virus is shed in feces. Lifelong immunity usually develops after infection with wild hepatitis virus or vaccination with inactivated virus.

More foodborne outbreaks of disease have been attributed to hepatitis A virus than any other virus (Jay 2000). Many of these outbreaks are caused by contaminated shellfish, which play a unique role in the transmission of the virus. Many shellfish are harvested from waters impacted by treated and untreated sewage effluents containing hepatitis A virus. Shellfish concentrate hepatitis A viruses in their tissues as they filter-feed. Thus, contaminated shellfish may contain high levels of hepatitis A virus. In addition to shellfish, hepatitis A virus has been isolated from a variety of foods including green onions and milk. Contamination of food in these cases may occur from indirect fecal-oral contact, namely from contaminated hands coming into contact with food. Because viruses cannot replicate outside of living host cells, lack of refrigeration will not result in increased concentrations of viruses in food.

Foodborne parasites

Although parasites exhibit remarkable variation in terms of their life cycles, transmission through food is marked by one of two main mechanisms. In the first, environmentally resistant parasites such as the protozoa *Giardia lamblia* and *Cryptosporidium parvum* contaminate food indirectly by fecal contamination of meats during butchering or preparation. In the second, parasites such as *Sarcocystis hominis* and *Trichinella spiralis* encyst in the meat of animals and are consumed by humans. After being ingested, the parasites excyst, multiply, and travel to other tissues where they can form new, persistent cysts. This mechanism of foodborne parasite transmission may result in debilitating disease and is associated with muscle pain, fever, and sometimes neurological complications.

Because they may reside in the intestines or muscles of many meat animals, animal parasites represent a major, but often undiagnosed, source of foodborne disease. There are many foodborne parasites with unique ecologies and it is beyond the scope of this book to examine each one in detail. Many different foodborne parasites can cause foodborne infections (See Table 8.1). Parasites may contaminate many types of food.

Because many parasites are found in environmentally resistant states, such as in cysts, thorough cooking is the only dependable way to remove them from food. Numbers of cysts in meat can be greatly reduced by assuring that the food for meat animals, especially the carcasses of other animals, is kept free from parasite contamination.

Table 8.1
Common Foodborne Parasites and Disease

Microorganism	Disease: Symptoms	Likely Source in Food
Cryptosporidium parvum	Cryptosporidiosis: Profuse diarrhea, nausea, vomiting.	Shellfish, fecally contaminated meats, especially beef.
Cyclospora cayetanensis	Cyclosporiasis: Diarrhea, fatigue.	Various, raspberries and lettuce have been implicated.
Giardia lamblis	Giardiasis: Profuse, persistent diarrhea, abdominal cramps, fatigue.	Various, fecally contaminated meat and vegetables have been implicated.
Sarcocystis hominis, *S. suihominis*	Sarcocystosis: Headache, diarrhea, nausea.	Contaminated, undercooked beef or pork.
Taenia saginata, *T. solium*	Cysticercosis: Generally asymptomatic, muscle pain, neurological complications.	Contaminated, undercooked beef or pork.
Toxoplasma gondii	Toxoplasmosis: Abortion in pregnant women, fever, muscle pain, rash, swelling of lymph nodes.	Contaminated, undercooked meat, especially beef, pork, and mutton. Fecal contamination may occur from cat feces.
Trichinella spiralis	Trichinosis: Diarrhea, nausea, vomiting, muscle pain, and difficulty breathing in severe cases.	Contaminated, undercooked meat, especially pork.

8.8 Chapter Summary

Foodborne transmission of disease is a major concern in the United States. Foodborne illness can be brought about by ingestion of preformed toxins or by infection of the intestines by foodborne microorganisms. Pathogens may be present on many types of raw foods. Other foods become contaminated during handling, processing, or food service. In some cases, a contaminant present at the source is mishandled and multiplies in food. Other times, tainted foods contaminate foods that are eaten raw. Meat and poultry manufacturers are required to use the HACCP system to reduce levels of pathogens in food and other manufacturers do so voluntarily. The HACCP system is based on microbial monitoring of critical points during processing to control the overall risk of contamination. A relatively small subset of microorganisms is responsible for the vast majority of foodborne illness. The microorganisms responsible for the greatest amount of foodborne illness in the developed world include *Salmonella*, *E. coli*, *Campylobacter*, *Shigella*, noroviruses, and the protozoan parasites *Giardia* and *Cryptosporidium*. Foodborne disease claims can be substantiated by epidemiological investigations or by showing the presence of the pathogen in the food, person, or both through diagnostic microbiology or the testimony of expert witnesses.

Chapter 9

Airborne Microbial Diseases

Synopsis

9.1 Chapter Preview

This chapter discusses the role that aerosolized microorganisms play in disease transmission and gives examples of common airborne pathogens. The vehicles for pathogen transport, called bioaerosols, are also described. This chapter outlines some of the more problematic environmental microorganisms that are spread through air. Mold-associated diseases including toxic-mold syndrome are considered with a focus on the plausibility of mold injury claims and descriptions of the proposed mechanisms of mold injury. Some of the fungal diseases that have become important with respect to AIDS are also outlined. *Legionella* bacteria, which are a problem in air conditioners and spas, are discussed with a focus on the role that disinfectants play in preventing transmission. By reading this chapter, lawyers and judges will learn about airborne disease transmission in general and about specific pathogens and activities of concern. In addition, this chapter provides legal professionals with an up-to-date scientific perspective regarding toxic mold and associated legal issues.

9.2 Introduction

Many infectious diseases are transmitted through air, including colds, the flu, Legionnaire's Disease, tuberculosis, and a variety of fungal lung infections. Although many airborne diseases are mild, some can cause deadly pandemics. For example, in 1918 the Spanish Flu spread throughout the United States and the world. The pandemic was so severe that in the United States it killed about 900,000 people. The worldwide death toll from the Spanish flu was around 25 million people in just one year. The Spanish Flu pandemic was due to the emergence of a new strain of the flu with increased virulence and a reservoir of people who had never been exposed to the virus. The seriousness of airborne diseases was highlighted more recently in 1976 when war veterans attending a convention in Philadelphia became victims of a mysterious, pneumonia-like disease. A total of 182 people became ill and twenty-nine died. An intensive investigation revealed that a newly discovered bacterium, now known as *Legionella pneumophila*, was the cause of the disease. It had been spread through aerosols from a contaminated air conditioning unit. Aerosols also transmit the bacterium that causes the lung disease tuberculosis. Tuberculosis is prevalent throughout the world and is of particular concern in hospitals. In addition to bacteria and viruses, certain fungi can infect the lungs through bioaerosols. Airborne fungi such as *Aspergillus* and *Pneumocystis* are a major problem for those suffering from AIDS.

During the 1980s and 1990s, aerobiologists focused on pathogens transmitted to humans through air from environmental sources such as cooling towers, wastewater treatment facilities, and areas where wastewater was sprayed onto land for irrigation. Risky operations were identified and measures were taken to prevent outbreaks. Since then, the aerosol research landscape has changed. Outdoor aerosol studies now focus on concentrated animal feeding operations such as swine houses and dairies where there are concerns that diseases may be transmitted to humans. Studies also now take place in the indoor environment.

Many people are concerned about adverse health effects from black or toxic mold, known scientifically as *Stachybotrys chartarum*. Like many other molds, *Stachybotrys chartarum* can grow in moist environments including on drywall and carpeting that has gotten wet. Unlike many other molds, however, Stachybotrys *chartarum* produces a potent neurotoxin, which is contained in spores and fungal fragments. When administered in purified form to laboratory animals in high doses, this toxin causes seizures and even death. As a result, many people are concerned about the potential for illness caused by inhalation of airborne *Stachybotrys chartarum* spores. Those claiming to have been injured by mold toxins often complain of pulmonary dysfunction, asthma, allergies, chemical pneumonitis, headache, rash, mental disorientation, memory loss, and multiple chemical sensitivity (Herz 2005).

9.3 Bioaerosols

A biological aerosol (bioaerosol), is an airborne particle, either dry or in a liquid suspension, that contains a microorganism or part thereof. Biological aerosols can originate from many sources, ranging from water in ornamental fountains to fungi living in soil. One of the best examples of bioaerosol generation is an uncovered sneeze by someone with a cold or flu. When someone sneezes, thousands of tiny droplets of respiratory fluid are carried by air out of the lungs, through the nasal passages, and into the environment. Once a bioaerosol is created, it floats around for some time, depending on its weight, size, and electrical charge. If a potential host inhales it, the microorganism can infect respiratory tissue and repeat the cycle of infection.

Whether or not inhalation of a bioaerosol will result in infection depends, in part, on the size of the bioaerosol droplets. Because the airway is curved and traveling bioaerosol droplets have momentum, those that are large (ten microns in diameter or more) are more likely to impact the back of the throat when they are inhaled and then be swallowed. Conversely, bioaerosols that are small (five microns in diameter or less) are more likely to make it to the narrow tubules of the lungs, where they impact lung tissue. This suggests that the aerosol route may occasionally spread enteric pathogens, such as *Salmonella*, if the pathogens are contained in larger bioaerosols. It also suggests that a respiratory pathogen is most likely to cause an infection if it resides in a smaller aerosol since it will likely travel further into the lung.

Touching a surface that has been contaminated by microorganisms that were once in an aerosol that settled out of the atmosphere can also spread disease. The likelihood of this type of disease transmission is lower than through direct transmission by aerosols, however, because microorganisms on surfaces may be more attracted to the surface they land on than to the hand that touches the surface, resulting in a low carryover rate to the hand. They must then be transmitted from the hand to the mouth for this type of spread, which is not very efficient.

Bioaerosols rarely cause disease at great distances from the source because most microorganisms do not survive well within bioaerosols. Ultraviolet light, dessication, and changes in temperature all contribute to die-off (Brooks 2004). In addition, dispersion of bioaerosols from the source results in lower concentrations at greater distances, reducing the likelihood of exposure to a great number of microorganisms all at once. Certain bacterial and fungal spores have evolved to be resistant to many environmental effects and can persist for long periods of time in bioaerosols.

Some bioaerosols do not contain live microorganisms at all, but can still cause disease. Illness from these aerosols is caused by exposure to airborne biological toxins. The most common biological toxin on earth (and in the air) is called lipopolysaccharide (LPS), or endotoxin. This toxin is present on the surface of gram-negative bacteria and is known to produce asthma-like symptoms if large quantities are inhaled. If small quantities of endotoxin enter the bloodstream, fever will usually result. In cases of extreme exposure to airborne endotoxin, shock and death have been reported. Endotoxin is a ubiquitous contaminant of air, water, and food. For this reason, airborne endotoxin represents no threat to people who have normal exposure levels. Elevated exposure levels can be found among those who work with compost or in agriculture (Clark 1983). Certain fungi also produce toxins, called mycotoxins, which may be detected in air. Depending on the type of mycotoxin, a variety of symptoms of disease may develop, ranging in severity from allergy-like conditions to respiratory failure. As with endotoxin, exposure to fungal toxins must be extreme to cause disease.

9.4 Diseases from Outdoor Air

Although many diseases have the potential to be transmitted through outdoor air, very few are likely to cause litigation. For example, colds and the flu are transmitted outside from time to time, but people regard these diseases as a normal part of life. Negligent transmission of such diseases is considered to be more socially reprehensible than illegal.

One potential source of disease in outdoor air is wastewater treatment facilities, which are present in most communities, often near population centers. Scientists have measured pathogen aerosolization rates at wastewater treatment facilities. One study demonstrated that total coliform concentrations ranged from 1.0 to 1,138 bacteria per cubic meter of air at these facilities. The same study showed that wastewater treatment workers might come in contact with concentrations as high as 31.6 enteroviruses per cubic meter of air in certain parts of a wastewater treatment plant (Carducci 2000). However, concern about aerosols from wastewater treatment plants has been largely muted by epidemiological studies, which have tracked infection rates in sewage treatment plant workers and generally did not find increased rates of disease. The working theory is that if those who work around aerosols do not demonstrate any more illness than those who do not, then the risk to the public from lower doses of the same bioaerosols must be minimal. In general, studies agree that aerosol emissions from wastewater treatment facilities do not cause disease in the community.

Certain agricultural operations may generate bioaerosols outdoors but these bioaerosols are not likely to spread disease to communities. For example, farmers use tractors to spread human and animal waste on land as a fertilizer throughout the United States. Tractors fling the waste, in small clumps, through the air in order to spread it evenly on the land. Class B biosolids, which are the principal type of human waste applied to land, contain a variety of enteric pathogens. The United States Environmental Protection Agency (USEPA) estimates that 6.9 million dry tons of Class B biosolids are generated in the United States each year. Federal regulations stipulate that Class B biosolids contain fewer than 2 million fecal coliforms per dry gram. Between 2002 and 2005, researchers at the University of Arizona undertook a nationwide study of bioaerosol generation during biosolids application, eventually quantifying the risk to biosolids applicators and to communities downwind of land application sites. They determined that workers are subject to a small annual risk of infection, but risks to communities as a result of this practice are insignificant (Brooks 2004, Tanner 2006). Pathogen aerosolization from animal waste is likely to be associated with greater risks because animal waste is not commonly treated to reduce pathogen levels. Unfortunately, a nationwide study of the risk to communities and workers resulting from land application of animal wastes has not yet been reported.

9.5 Diseases from Indoor Air

Aside from the countless instances of cold and flu transmission through indoor air, which are rarely litigated, there are only a few diseases of concern that can be transmitted via indoor aerosols. These include tuberculosis, Legionnaire's Disease, and a few fungal lung infections that can cause illness in the immunocompromised. However, certain mold-related illnesses, including Toxic Mold Syndrome, Sick Building Syndrome, and Building-Related Illness are frequently litigated, whether there is scientific evidence for airborne transmission of mold diseases or not.

Mycobacterium tuberculosis is a bacterium that causes tuberculosis and is spread through indoor aerosols. The only known reservoir of this pathogen is other infected humans. Tuberculosis infects a large number of people throughout the world and is a major airborne pathogen. In the United States, approximately 20,000 new infections occur each year and approximately 2,000 people die from tuberculosis (Brock 2000). The most effective way to prevent the spread of tuberculosis is to identify those who are infected (using the simple tuberculin skin test) and prevent them from having unnecessary contact with large numbers of susceptible people.

Legionnaires' disease and Pontiac fever are respiratory infections that result from *Legionella* bacteria in aerosols from improperly disinfected whirlpools, spas and air conditioners (as described in Chapter 7). Infection by *Legionella* bacteria can be quite serious, and is strongly associated with negligent disinfection practices. Many cases have been described in hotels and other public places, although litigation involving *Legionella* is not particularly common.

Certain fungi, such as the opportunistic pathogens *Aspergillus fumigatus* and *Pneumocystis carinii* can infect the lungs of the immunocompromised, including AIDS patients. Symptoms of infection may include fever, cough, chest pain, and pneumonia. These fungi most commonly originate from soil and are very common in the environment. Nonetheless, care should be taken not to transmit these pathogens through indoor air to susceptible individuals.

A great deal of indoor airborne disease litigation stems from contamination of homes by mold. Mold in homes is clearly negative in many ways: It is unsightly, it degrades furniture and walls, and it is malodorous. In some cases, mold litigation focuses on the negative aesthetic qualities of the mold, such as when a homebuyer detects mold staining in a new house before moving in. However, most claimants, and especially those who live in mold-damaged homes, tend to cite health injuries from mold toxins as a reason for litigation. They usually describe their mold injury in a manner such as follows:

> I moved into the home two years ago, and began to have severe headaches and muscle pain soon thereafter. After living in the home for three months, I noticed extensive mold contamination of the bedroom drywall after removing some stained wallpaper, and later found mold growing in my living room and in my bedroom closet. I hired a microbiologist to examine the mold, who told me that my home had millions of spores of the toxin-producing fungus *Stachybotrys chartarum*. Since living in the house I have become ill, and I'm sure my illness (toxic mold syndrome) is a direct result of contact with toxin-containing spores from the fungus.

An entire industry now exists offering mold detection, identification and remediation, but whether or not *Stachybotrys chartarum* actually causes illness is questionable. Certainly, some of the toxins produced by *Stachybotrys chartarum* are capable of causing harm to humans in very high doses and there is no doubt that *Stachybotrys chartarum* grows in some homes. Nevertheless, a compelling dose-response model has yet to be generated for low-level exposures (even for animals) and studies have yet to be performed to assess the amount of *Stachybotrys chartarum* actually inhaled by an occupant of a mold-contaminated home under normal circumstances. Additionally, *Stachybotrys chartarum* does not always produce the toxins that are suspected to cause injury and its spores require extensive mechanical agitation to become airborne. At this point, scientific evidence suggests that mold in homes is not responsible for anything except for mold-related allergic reactions.

Another variety of indoor airborne disease litigation involves sick-building syndrome and building-related illness. These diseases are similar in terms of perceived causation and symptoms to toxic mold syndrome, but center on community buildings such as office complexes and apartment buildings. Like toxic mold syndrome, those who claim to be afflicted by sick-building syndrome report a wide variety of non-specific symptoms ranging from headache to fatigue. Those who suffer from building-related illness tend to mention more specific symptoms, like asthma. Those who suffer from these diseases speculate that a wide variety of biological pollutants in the air are the cause, including live and dead bacteria and fungi in air ducts or mold toxins. Air handling systems are a commonly implicated source of indoor air pollution. Problems may be reported because there is little or no air circulation, the environment is very dusty, or because air handling systems are poorly maintained. While there is no question that exposure to mold fragments and spores result in allergies, there is currently no evidence to suggest that airborne mold toxins have serious impacts on the health of those who claim to suffer from sick building syndrome and building related illness. Lawyers and judges with special interest in litigation stemming from mold issues can find additional information in *Toxic Mold Litigation* (Herz 2005).

In addition to injury from mold, airborne endotoxin is sometimes cited as a cause of illness in buildings. Endotoxin is another word for Lipid A, which is found on the surface of gram-negative bacteria as part of a structure called lipopolysaccharide (LPS). If endotoxin enters the bloodstream in sufficient doses, it can cause fever, diarrhea, and vomiting. If inhaled, it can result in asthma-like symptoms. The endotoxin argument is generally structured as follows:

> Endotoxins are scientifically accepted as causes of nonspecific illness, and I was exposed to an excessive amount of endotoxins in my building over an extended period of time because air ducts were never cleaned and filters were never replaced, exposing me to endotoxin containing dust each day for years.

However, a key property of endotoxin is that, like bacteria, it is everywhere. To successfully argue that a nonspecific illness has been caused by endotoxin in a building's air, a litigant must show that endotoxin levels in the building are significantly higher than other common sources of exposure, such as in drinking water and outdoor air, which is unlikely.

9.6 Commonly Implicated Pathogens

Legionella pneumophila

Legionella are thin, gram-negative, rod-shaped bacteria with distinctive nutritional requirements, including an unusually high iron requirement (Brock 2000). When inhaled, *Legionella* cause a pneumonia-like illness called Legionnaires' disease and a similar, influenza-like disease called Pontiac fever. Legionnaires' disease is a serious infection largely affecting people fifty years old or older with 50 percent of hospitalized cases resulting in mortality. Pontiac fever is a much milder form of *Legionella* infection, in which all infected individuals recover. These bacteria are known to inhabit intracellular structures of higher microorganisms including protozoa, which may provide them with protection from the environment and disinfectants. *Legionella* bacteria are most frequently isolated from environmental sources between 35°C and 45°C, and are killed at temperatures above 60°C. Although they are common in the environment, *Legionella* only appear to be capable of causing disease in humans after growing at temperatures above 24°C (Mauchline et al. 1994).

Legionella bacteria can be isolated from many environmental sources. They are a key concern in cooling towers, drinking water distribution systems, air humidifiers, water fountains, outdoor misters, whirlpools, hot tubs, spas, hot water tanks and domestic hot water heaters. Because Legionnellosis is caused by inhalation of small droplets of water containing *Legionella*, the bubbling action of whirlpools or the evaporative action of air conditioners can increase the aerosolization of contaminated droplets and the threat of an individual developing Legionnaires' disease or Pontiac fever.

Mycobacterium tuberculosis

The bacterium that causes tuberculosis is known scientifically as *Mycobacterium tuberculosis*. It is loosely rod-shaped and does not respond to gram-staining. Instead, it can be identified by its tendency to absorb a particular stain or by its "acid-fastness."

Mycobacterium tuberculosis is also unique among human pathogens because of its very slow growth rate. After infecting the lungs, *Mycobacterium tuberculosis* are able to persist for long periods of time. The immune systems copes with the infection by surrounding colonies of bacteria with groups of immune cells called macrophages. The clumps of immune cells surrounding the bacteria are called tubercules. Tubercules contain the infection, but do not necessarily kill the *Mycobacteria*. In many cases, bacteria that have been controlled for long periods of time are reactivated by some event that depresses the immune system, such as aging or infection with HIV.

Mycobacterium tuberculosis is a major human pathogen due to its special characteristics and propensity for airborne transmission. Tuberculosis is prevalent worldwide and approximately 20,000 new cases are reported each year in the United States (Brock 2000). Tuberculosis can be treated with antibiotics but infections take approximately one year of daily medication to cure. As a result, many infected people do not complete treatment, resulting in antibiotic resistance. In addition to the difficulty with treatment, many people are infected with *Mycobacterium tuberculosis* for years without ever showing signs of infection. These people serve as dangerous reservoirs of *Mycobacterium tuberculosis* in the community. In an attempt to prevent the spread of tuberculosis, health care workers are screened for previous exposure to *Mycobacterium tuberculosis* with tuberculin skin tests. If positive, they may be required to take antibiotics to treat any potential infections or may be barred from patient contact. Tuberculosis remains a key challenge for those seeking to stop indoor transmission of airborne diseases.

Influenza viruses

Influenza viruses are enveloped (membrane-covered) viruses, which use ribonucleic acid (RNA) as their genetic blueprint and cause the flu. Influenza viruses infect the cells in the respiratory tract. Once infection is initiated, millions of viral progeny are produced. Progeny are then transmitted to other hosts by aerosolization in small droplets of respiratory and nasal fluid generated during coughing and sneezing. Influenza virus has a reasonably high rate of mutation.

The flu is characterized by annual infection cycles, seasonal variation in the number of infections, and the potential for pandemic outbreaks. Influenza usually affects the United States during the winter. Every forty or so years, an especially virulent strain of influenza arises. This occurred most dramatically during the Spanish Flu pandemic of 1918, when nearly a million people were killed during one year in the United States. Because influenza viruses mutate in a somewhat predictable fashion, each year microbiologists analyze the global set of influenza virus strains to predict the traits of next year's strain and to produce vaccines. However, influenza vaccines are only effective if the virus mutates as predicted, which is about three-quarters of the time. Because they are covered in a delicate fatty structure called the viral envelope, disinfectant chemicals can inactivate influenza viruses relatively easily. Thus, hygienic precautions such as covering coughs and sneezes and disinfecting potentially contaminated surfaces help to prevent the spread of influenza virus infections.

Rhinovirus

Rhinoviruses are the primary cause of the common cold. Rhinoviruses are members of the virus family *Picornaviridae*, meaning that they are extremely small (approximately twenty-two nanometers in diameter), use RNA as their genetic blueprint and lack a fatty viral membrane. Rhinoviruses are predominantly spread through aerosols generated by coughs and sneezes, but contaminated surfaces may also play a role in transmission.

Rhinovirus infection is rarely confirmed in the laboratory because infections are usually mild and viral infections are costly to confirm. As a result, the true prevalence of rhinovirus disease is unknown. Like influenza viruses, rhinoviruses follow a seasonal pattern of transmission, with the United States, observing most cases in the fall and winter.

Stachybotrys chartarum

Although many species of indoor mold produce toxins and many are black, *Stachybotrys chartarum*, known as black mold or toxic mold, is by far the most infamous. This fungus grows preferentially in dark, humid environments and is damp to the touch. It sustains itself by degrading the cellulose constituents of indoor walls and furnishings. *Stachybotrys chartarum* is capable of producing toxins under certain growth conditions, including a potent neurological toxin. Unlike some other fungal species, the spores of *Stachybotrys chartarum* do not become airborne easily.

Scientists have not yet determined which factors contribute to toxin production in homes and buildings. If *Stachybotrys chartarum* is allowed to dry, mechanical disturbance of contaminated walls and furnishings may aerosolize *Stachybotrys chartarum* spores and hyphae (small, hair-like structural components of mold). Although toxins from *Stachybotrys chartarum* have been shown to cause disease in laboratory animals at high doses, the link between actual levels of airborne exposure to *Stachybotrys chartarum* and disease is tenuous at best. At this point, the major threat from *Stachybotrys chartarum* comes from its allergenic and aesthetic properties.

Aspergillus

Aspergillus is a large and diverse genus of fungi, containing approximately 200 species. *Aspergillus* is commonly found in soil, on plants, and in the air. If inhaled, certain species of *Aspsergillus* can colonize and invade the lungs of susceptible individuals. Most commonly, exposure to the mold causes allergic reactions.

The prevalence of *Aspergillus* infections is not well understood although studies suggest that agricultural workers are at a higher risk of infection. The biggest risks from this mold come from certain species of *Aspergillus* known to infect the immunocompromised, including *As-*

pergillus flavus and *Aspergillus fumigatus*. The risk associated with *Aspergillus* infection is particularly high in late-stage AIDS patients. The prevalence of allergy caused by *Aspergillus* is poorly understood and it is viewed primarily as a nuisance.

Coccidioides immitis

Coccidioides immitis is a fungus that lives in the desert soils of the Southwestern United States. If spores of this fungus are inhaled, the fungus can germinate in the in the lungs and invade surrounding tissue, causing a disease known as Valley Fever, or coccidioidomycosis. Coccidioidomycosis is associated with fever, coughing, and sometimes pneumonia.

Coccidioides immitis infection is strongly associated with exposure to fungal aerosols from soil. This is of particular concern in places where soil dust is generated in large quantities near population centers. For example, during construction or demolition at southwestern college campuses, large quantities of soil-borne fungi may be aerosolized within yards of thousands of students. Many people living in the Southwest show signs of previous infections by this fungus, although most probably assumed that they had a cold or the flu. Infections with *Coccidioides immitis* may be deadly in those suffering from AIDS. As a result, dust-abatement efforts are commonly used in the Southwest to help reduce new cases of coccidioidomycosis.

9.7 Chapter Summary

Aerosols can transmit many diseases. Pathogenic microorganisms travel through air in the form of bioaerosols, which are subject to degradation by the environment and must reach a susceptible host to initiate infection. Seasonal colds and the flu are the most commonly transmitted airborne diseases, but they are not commonly litigated and are considered to be a normal part of life. Tuberculosis is an airborne disease that can be spread from person to person and is responsible for a great number of infections and deaths in the United States. Legionnaire's disease is transmitted via the aerosol route and can be spread by improper disinfection of swimming pools and water-based air conditioners. Several fungal lung infections can also be spread through air. Some can be prevented by proper dust abatement during soil agitation. Some of the most interesting airborne diseases are toxic mold syndrome, sick building syndrome, and building-related illness, in which people claim to have been injured by mold toxins spread through air from mold-contaminated furnishings and other building structures. A method to detect exposure to mold toxins and a solid dose-response relationship has yet to be developed for the mold species named in nearly all cases, *Stachybotrys chartarum*, so litigating such claims remains a challenge.

Chapter 10

Body-fluid and Insect-borne Diseases

Synopsis

10.1 Chapter Preview

Although there are many bloodborne, insect-borne and sexually transmitted diseases, only a few result in litigation in the United States. This chapter discusses bloodborne diseases, focusing on the diseases those can be spread by blood transfusions. Insect-borne diseases are also explored, including the emerging insect-borne pathogen West Nile virus. Finally, a wide variety of sexually transmitted diseases are discussed, with special attention given to HIV, the cause of AIDS. This chapter provides lawyers and judges with a starting point for the somewhat rare but very important cases involving bloodborne, insect-borne, and sexually transmitted diseases.

10.2 Introduction

A variety of infectious diseases are spread by pathogens in blood, sexual fluids, and insects (See Table 10.1). In general, bloodborne and sexually transmitted diseases circulate globally, while insect-borne diseases are limited to the geographic regions where the pathogen-carrying insects live. With the exception of malaria, which is caused by a parasite and spread by mosquitoes, bacteria and viruses cause nearly all fluid and insect-borne diseases. Bacteria are significant sexually transmitted disease agents because some adhere tightly to reproductive cells and are efficiently transmitted through sex. Bacteria are an important source of insect- borne infections. Many types of viruses cause fluid and insect-borne diseases. Viruses are significant because very few are required to initiate infection and because great numbers can be present in the blood and sexual fluid of infected people.

Fluid and insect-borne diseases are a major problem in developing countries because of limited availability of antibiotics, pesticides, regional geography, and level of education. The most important reason for lower rates of fluid and insect-borne diseases in first world countries is access to drugs and pesticides that control fluid and insect-borne diseases. Regional geography plays an important role because most insect-borne diseases are limited to the regions where disease-transmitting insects can survive. For example, in climates suitable for *Anopheles*, the mosquito that transmits malaria, malaria is a major disease. In these areas, over 100 million people are currently infected with malaria and around a million die each year (Brock 2000). Since the advent of HIV, the disparity between disease rates in developed and developing countries has been increasingly associated with the level of education. For example, HIV was originally discovered among homosexuals and intravenous drug abusers in San Francisco in the United States, but AIDS education initiatives discouraging unsafe sex and needle sharing slowed the HIV outbreak in that region. In contrast, Africans (including African health care workers) were largely uneducated about the spread of HIV and as a result the virus spread quickly throughout Africa.

In the United States, the most important fluid and insect-borne pathogens are hepatitis B and C viruses, HIV, West Nile Virus, and the bacterium that causes Lyme disease. Hepatitis B and C viruses are an issue in developed countries because they can be spread through sex, intravenous drug abuse, and blood transfusions. Infection with these viruses causes hepatitis, liver cirrhosis, and liver cancer. HIV is arguably the most important fluid-borne virus in the United States today, although less than one percent of the population is infected. HIV can be controlled almost entirely by through basic preventative measures.

Table 10.1
Fluid and Insect-borne Pathogens

Pathogen	Type of Microbe	Transmission	Disease
Borrelia burgdorferi	Bacterium	Tick	Lyme Disease
Chlamidia trachomatis	Bacterium	Sexual Contact	Urinary Tract Infection, Reproductive Damage
Erlichia	Bacterium	Tick	Rash, Fever
Neisseria gonorrhea	Bacterium	Sexual Contact	Urinary Tract Infection, Reproductive Damage
Rickettsia rickettsii	Bacterium	Tick	Rocky Mountain Spotted Fever
Treponema pallidum	Bacterium	Sexual Contact	Syphilis
Yersinia pestis	Bacterium	Flea	Bubonic Plague
Plasmodium	Parasite	Mosquito	Malaria
Trichomonas vaginalis	Parasite	Sexual Contact	Urinary Tract Infections
Dengue Virus	Virus	Mosquito	High Fever, Hemorrhaging
Ebola Virus	Virus	Blood	High Fever, Hemorrhaging
Hepatitis B Virus	Virus	Sexual Contact, Blood	Hepatitis, Liver Cancer
Hepatitis C Virus	Virus	Sexual Contact, Blood	Hepatitis, Liver Cirrhosis
Herpesvirus Type 2	Virus	Sexual Contact	Herpes
Human Immunodeficiency Virus (HIV)	Virus	Blood, Sexual Contact, Birth	Acquired Immunodeficiency Syndrome (AIDS)
Human T-cell Lymphotrophic Virus	Virus	Blood, Sexual Contact, Birth	Leukemia, Lymphoma
Monkeypox	Virus	Blood	Rash, Difficulty Breathing
Papillomavirus	Virus	Sexual Contact	Warts
Rabies Virus	Virus	Animal Bite	Rabies
West Nile Virus	Virus	Mosquito	Meningitis, Encephalitis
Yellow Fever Virus	Virus	Mosquito	Fever, Pain, Nausea, Vomiting

Since humans can take simple actions to control the spread of hepatitis B, C, and HIV, negligent transmission of these viruses can be a source of litigation. Blood transfusions can be a source of litigation when blood is not screened properly for viral contamination. HIV infections are also litigated. Because the public is generally knowledgeable about the spread and effects of HIV, some claimants have won damages after being infected with HIV through sex with someone who knew that they were infected with the virus, but declined to inform their partner. In contrast to fluid-borne diseases, insect-borne diseases are rarely litigated.

10.3 Bloodborne Diseases

Bloodborne diseases are those that are transmitted through contaminated blood. However, it is doubtful that any pathogens have evolved specifically to be transferred directly from the blood of one person to another. Thus, it is more appropriate to consider all bloodborne diseases more broadly as fluid-borne diseases. For some pathogens, a large percentage of total disease transmission may come from blood-to-blood contact through transfusions and intravenous drug abuse.

The most notorious bloodborne pathogen is hepatitis B virus, which is notable because it is highly contagious. Health care professionals who maintain records of "needlestick" accidents provide data that supports this. A needlestick occurs when a healthcare worker accidentally punctures himself or herself with a needle used previously on a patient with a bloodborne disease. The data show that needlesticks from hepatitis B patients are approximately ten times more likely to transmit disease than needlesticks from HIV patients. Hepatitis C virus and HIV are also important. HIV and hepatitis C virus are spread in the same way as hepatitis B virus. These pathogens are especially common among homosexuals and intravenous drug abusers in the United States.

Bloodborne diseases can be controlled by reducing intravenous drug abuse and screening blood transfusions for bloodborne microorganisms whenever possible. In addition, hepatitis B virus infections can be prevented by vaccination. Currently, no cures or vaccines exist for hepatitis C virus or HIV, so prevention of these infections depends on screening blood for transfusion, using sterile or disposable medical instruments, and minimizing unprotected sex and intravenous drug abuse.

10.4 Insect-borne Diseases

Insect-borne diseases arise when an insect contaminated with pathogens bites or otherwise infects a human. In the cycle of disease transmission, the insect is referred to as the vector. For most insect-borne diseases, a particular species of insect acts as the disease vector. This imposes distinct geographical boundaries for many insect-borne diseases, and means that if a person becomes infected with an insect-borne disease in one region and takes the infection to a region lacking the vector, they are not likely to infect another person.

Insect-borne diseases are responsible for at least one million deaths per year worldwide, but are less of a concern in the United States. Important insect-borne diseases in the United States include Rocky Mountain spotted fever, Lyme disease, and West Nile fever. Lyme disease is caused by a spirochete bacterium, called *Borrelia burdoferi* which is transmitted from the blood of infected wildlife to the blood of humans through the bite of a tick. Lyme disease most often results in a characteristic rash that spreads radially from the bite wound, along with headache and fever. Although Lyme disease is rarely fatal, it can to produce serious sequelae if untreated, including visual disturbances, facial paralysis, seizures, and arthritis. Rocky Mountain spotted fever is a similar disease, but it is caused by a different bacterium called *Rickettsia* and is generally less severe. This disease produces a patchy rash and high fever that lasts for about two weeks without treatment. Disease produced by West Nile virus is much different than bacterial insect-borne diseases common in the United States. West Nile virus is spread from birds to humans by mosquitoes. Infection can cause fever, swelling of the brain, and death. The best way to control the spread of West Nile virus is to eliminate the insect vector. This is done by reducing sources of standing water in which mosquitoes breed and by treating endemic areas with insecticides.

The best way to control insect-borne diseases is to eliminate the insect vector. This type of intervention has been successful for malaria, yellow fever, and other insect-borne diseases. It is especially effective against mosquito-borne diseases like West Nile fever. For tick-borne diseases, however, this may not be practical. Thus, it is advisable for those in the outdoors, especially in endemic areas of disease, to wear insect repellants.

10.5 Sexually Transmitted Diseases

Sexually transmitted diseases are those that can be spread by sexual contact. Common sexually transmitted diseases include AIDS, genital herpes, syphilis, gonorrhea, chlamydia, genital warts, hepatitis B, and hepatitis C. HIV is a unique virus that attacks the cells of the immune system and is fatal in nearly all cases over extended periods of time. Genital herpes is a relatively mild infection caused by herpesvirus type 2, closely related to the cause of oral cold sores, herpesvirus type 1. Herpes is characterized by small ulcers that develop on the skin of infected areas. Ulcers caused by herpes viruses may appear as often as once a month or never at all. Syphilis is disease caused by the spirochete bacterium *Treponema pallidum* and is not common in the United States. If left untreated, this disease can result in open sores and neurological damage. Gonorrhea is a sexually transmitted disease caused by the bacterium *Neisseria gonorrhoeae*, common in the United States. Gonorrhea results primarily in irritation of the male urethra. Chlamydia is similar to gonorrhea, but is slightly more prevalent, more difficult to diagnose, and is caused by a different bacterium, called *Chlamydia trachomatis*. Genital warts are caused by papillomaviruses. Papillomavirus infections are linked to cervical cancer.

In the fifty or so years after the discovery of antibiotics, sexually transmitted diseases were regarded generally as inconsequential, easily treatable infections. Recently, however, AIDS has emerged and microbiologists have begun to recognize the potential for long-term effects from some sexually transmitted diseases caused by bacteria. The problem with HIV is clear; unlike most other pathogens, HIV is almost always fatal and has great potential to spread. Problems with other sexually transmitted diseases are just beginning to be understood. For example, infection with *Chlamydia trachomatis* usually results in urinary tract irritation in both men and women. However, chronic infection with this bacterium can damage fallopian tubes in women and testicles in men leading to infertility. Similarly, infection with *Neisseria gonorrhoeae* can be asymptomatic in women and normally results in urinary tract irritation in men. Chronic infections can lead to pelvic inflammatory syndrome in women and damage to heart valves and joint tissues in both genders.

The only infallible way to prevent sexual disease transmission is to abstain from sex. If abstaining from sex is not an option, physical barriers such as condoms help prevent sexual fluids from being transferred from one person to another during sex. In the future, vaccines may be available to prevent some of the more harmful sexually transmitted diseases. Efforts are currently underway to create effective vaccines against HIV and papillomaviruses.

10.6 Commonly Implicated Pathogens

Human Immunodeficiency Virus

Human Immunodeficiency Virus (HIV) is a member of a special class of viruses called retroviruses. Retroviruses are unique because they are the only form of life that transforms genetic material from RNA to DNA. All other organisms change genetic material from DNA to RNA. HIV is an enveloped virus, meaning that it is surrounded by a thin layer of fatty material. However, the viral envelope is relatively fragile, making HIV extremely sensitive to the environment. HIV can be transmitted through blood or sexual fluid and can be transmitted from mothers to fetuses during pregnancy.

HIV primarily infects the cells of the immune system, eventually resulting in AIDS. The immune cell most often infected is the CD4 T-lymphocyte, or "T-helper" cell. HIV infection follows a predictable pattern once initiated. After a lag period of between about one week and two months, the virus replicates rapidly in the bloodstream by infecting many T-helper cells. In the host, this period is characterized by fever. Then, for a period that can range from one year to around one decade, the immune system and the virus reach a state of equilibrium, where viral particles are not likely to be in the blood, but plenty of anti-HIV antibodies are present. During this phase of infection, HIV patients may not show symptoms of infection. In time, however, HIV overwhelms the immune system. During this last phase of infection, patients develop the disease acquired-immunodeficiency syndrome, or AIDS. AIDS is caused by a gradual, but drastic reduction in the number of circulating T-helper cells. As a result, AIDS patients become more susceptible to many diseases, including a host of diseases caused by opportunistic pathogens. Microorganisms that commonly infect those with AIDS include *Mycobacterium tuberculosis*, a variety of enteric bacteria including *Salmonella*, and a number of opportunistic parasites and fungi, including *Cryptosporidium parvum*, *Pneumocystis carinii*, *Toxoplasma gondii*, *Cryptococcus neoformans*, *Candida albicans*, and *Histoplasma capsulatum*.

HIV probably entered the human population sometime between 1950 and 1970 as a variant of a related immunodeficiency virus that infects chimpanzees. AIDS was recognized as a disease in 1981 and now infects around a million people in the United States and at least 40 million people worldwide. In addition, rates of HIV infection continue to increase rapidly in most underdeveloped areas of the world. By all accounts, HIV is an extremely successful emerging virus. Three main factors have contributed to HIV's rapid dissemination among humans. First, it is transmitted through sex. Second, HIV infections normally include a long period without symptoms when the virus can be transmitted between hosts without any indications of infection. Lastly, HIV mutates rapidly in the body. This provides the immune system with a constant test and makes the manufacture of vaccines and drugs against the microorganism challenging because there is a high likelihood that an HIV mutant within the body will be resistant to one or more treatments. This resistance will then be passed on to the next person who is infected.

Hepatitis B virus

Hepatitis B virus is a member of the family *Hepadnaviridae*. It is an enveloped virus that uses DNA as its genetic material. Hepatitis B virus is not known to persist outside of the body but is highly contagious when contained in fresh bodily fluids. Once the virus infects the liver, it replicates slowly or quickly, depending on several circumstances. When it replicates slowly, as measured by the amount of viral DNA that can be measured in the bloodstream, it is generally less severe than when it replicates quickly. Hepatitis B virus is transmitted through blood or sexual fluids and can be transmitted from mothers to fetuses during pregnancy.

Most infections are diagnosed by looking for a particular antigen from the virus in the bloodstream. Diagnosis can also be made by liver biopsy. The primary site of infection is the liver, where the virus integrates itself into liver cells. Infection with hepatitis B virus can cause hepatitis, liver cirrhosis, and liver cancer. People who develop chronic infections are much more likely to experience cirrhosis and cancer. In adults, most cases are acute, meaning that they do not result in chronic infection. In children, however, infections become chronic in up to 50 percent of cases. Risk factors for hepatitis B infection include intravenous drug use, homosexual sex, work in a healthcare setting, and hemodialysis. Infections can sometimes be prevented after accidental exposure (such as by a needlestick) by administration of intramuscular anti-hepatitis B antibodies. Chronic infection with hepatitis B can be treated by interferon, an antiviral medicine. A vaccine is available for hepatitis B virus that is highly recommended for those at high risk of infection, including health care workers.

Hepatitis C virus

Hepatitis C virus is a member of the viral family *Flaviviridae*. It uses RNA as its genetic material and is surrounded by a fatty envelope. Hepatitis C virus is not known to survive outside of the body for extended periods of time. During an infection, hepatitis C viruses can be found throughout the body and in the bloodstream, although the virus is only known to infect the cells of the liver.

Like hepatitis B infection, the incubation period for hepatitis C ranges from a week to five months. Infection reduces liver function and can cause liver cirrhosis and liver cancer. In general, the later in life a person contracts the virus, the less likely they are to become a chronic carrier. Approximately 4 million people in the United States are infected with hepatitis C virus. The main risk factor for hepatitis C infection is intravenous drug abuse. Approximately three-quarters of all intravenous drug abusers test positive for hepatitis C virus. Other risk factors include unprotected sex and unhygienic piercings or tattoos. Since blood for transfusions has been screened for hepatitis C virus since 1992, the risk of infection by blood transfusion is low. Interferon can help to reduce the viral load in the body of an infected person. There is currently no vaccine available to prevent hepatitis C infections.

West Nile virus

West Nile virus is a member of the viral family *Flaviviridae*. It uses RNA as its genetic material and is surrounded by a fatty coating. The virus is known to survive inside mosquitoes, birds, horses, and humans. As a member of the family *Flaviviridae*, the virus is sensitive to most disinfectant chemicals and is not particularly resistant to environmental degradation. It can be found in both temperate and tropical regions in conjunction with a few specific types of mosquitoes. The virus is normally transmitted from the blood of infected wild birds to humans through mosquitoes, although a few cases from blood transfusions have been documented.

West Nile fever is an emerging insect-borne disease that was first recognized in the United States in 1992. The virus was originally isolated a feverish woman in the West Nile region of Uganda in 1937. Since then, it has spread throughout Europe, Asia, the Middle East, and most recently into the United States. The number of infections in the United States remains low, with approximately 5,000 infections occurring per year. West Nile fever has an incubation period of around a week, followed by flu-like symptoms. Less than 5 percent of infected individuals go on to develop further symptoms, which can include inflammation of the brain and rapid onset of paralysis. There is currently no treatment for West Nile fever and a vaccine has not yet been created. Thus, control of West Nile virus depends mainly on killing its mosquito vector.

10.7 Chapter Summary

A wide variety of bloodborne, insect-borne, and sexually transmitted diseases circulate worldwide. In developed countries, diseases that are spread through sex, blood transfusions, and intravenous drug abuse present the greatest problem. Although pathogens have not adapted specifically to blood-to-blood transmission, some sexually transmitted viruses can easily be transmitted in this way. The most important bloodborne pathogens are hepatitis B and C viruses, and HIV. If blood for transfusions is not properly screened for these pathogens, serious diseases can spread. Insect-borne diseases also represent a problem in the United States because of emerging West Nile Virus infections and Lyme disease. Since no vaccines are available for these diseases, control of the insect vector is the best way to prevent the spread of disease. There are many sexually transmitted diseases that circulate in the United States today. The emergence of HIV and increasing knowledge about the long-term consequences of other sexually transmitted diseases make them a legal concern.

Chapter 11

Hospital-Acquired Infections

Synopsis

11.1 Chapter Preview

Hospital-acquired infections are a major source of litigation. Some infections are normal, acceptable side effects of medical treatment, but others are the result of negligence. One of the ways legal professionals can prepare for this type of litigation is to understand how infectious diseases are transmitted in the unique environment of hospitals. This chapter explores hospital disease transmission, with emphasis the role that antibiotic resistance plays in the outcome and spread of disease. Infections are grouped by body location to highlight relevant medical treatments and potential sources of infection. Risk factors are identified for infections of the urinary tract, lungs, gastrointestinal tract, and bloodstream. Handwashing and disinfection are discussed as proven infection control measures. Finally, information is provided for each of the microorganisms that cause the majority of hospital-acquired infections.

11.2 Introduction

Hospital-acquired infections are common and expensive. In fact, approximately 10 percent of patients can expect to acquire an infection during their hospital stay (Filetoth 2003). Infections from hospitals range from easily treatable annoyances to treatment-resistant, severe diseases. If a patient acquires an infection while hospitalized, treatment costs are, on average, $2,100 higher. When a hospital patient acquires an infection of the bloodstream, their hospital stay is extended by seven days, on average, at a cost of approximately $3,500, in 1992 prices (Martone 1992).

Many factors facilitate pathogen transmission in hospitals. (See Table 11.1) Hospitals contain many infected people in general and there are a whole host of person-to-person and person-to-object interactions. In addition, hospitals are constantly receiving and discharging new patients, doctors and staff work irregular shifts, and most supplies are either disposable or sterilized between uses. Infectious disease transmission in hospitals is compounded by the fact that the most relevant hospital pathogens, like *Staphylococcus aureus*, can be spread in many ways and can infect many different parts of the body.

Hospitals are at the center of an infectious disease transmission cycle; people enter hospitals with community-acquired infections seeking treatment, and people exit with hospital-acquired infections, taking them into the community. Pathogens enter hospitals from the community on the bodies of infected patients and through air, food, and water. Once a pathogen enters a hospital, it may persist in the environment of the hospital or in the bodies of patients, staff and visitors. If a pathogen originally from the community is capable of creating an infection cycle within a hospital, it may adapt to the hospital environment and become a problematic hospital pathogen. For example, an environmental strain of *Pseudomonas aeruginosa* may be predisposed to sticking to hands. In a hospital, it could initiate a disease transmission cycle by resisting handwashing, being transferred to burn wounds by caretakers, then growing in wounds and recontaminating caretakers' hands. Once an infection cycle has been initiated in a hospital, it can be difficult to contain and may result in sporadic infections being transmitted to the community.

One of the biggest obstacles to infection control in hospitals is the disproportionate circulation of antibiotic resistant pathogens in hospital patients and the hospital environment. An infection acquired in a hospital is more likely to be resistant to antibiotics than an infection acquired anywhere else. Antibiotic resistant pathogens thrive in hospitals because antibiotics are a constant selective force there. That means that over time, the microorganisms that tend to survive antibiotic insults will proliferate and become more numerous. An argument is frequently made that appropriate antibiotic use will not result in antibiotic resistance, but this only applies to the microorganism targeted for destruction. Even when antibiotics are used properly against a particular infecting microorganism, they still act on other microorganisms in and on the body, often at sub-lethal levels and especially during the repetitive antibiotic treatments common with hospital patients. As a result, the general level of antibiotic resistance in hospital patients, and therefore hospitals, tends to rise over time. In the past, antibiotic resistance was only a problem with bacteria, but certain fungi and viruses, including HIV, now demonstrate resistance to antimicrobial drugs.

Table 11.1
Factors that Facilitate Transmission of Hospital-Acquired Pathogens

Pathogen	Characteristics Facilitating Hospital Transmission
Staphylococcus aureus	Part of normal human skin and gut flora, resistant to dry environments, certain strains resistant to broad spectrum of antibiotics.
Pseudomonas aeruginosa	Environmentally ubiquitous pathogen, naturally resistant to many antibiotics, physical characteristics provide resistance to chemical disinfectants, simple nutrient requirements for growth.
E. coli	Part of normal human gut flora, potential production of profuse diarrhea, certain strains have structures which allow bacterium to bind tightly to urinary epithelium.
Enterococcus faecalis	Major member of human gut flora, certain strains demonstrate antibiotic resistance to Vancomycin, somewhat resistant to dry environments.
Candida albicans	Part of normal human oral and vaginal flora, potential production of invasive hyphae, successful in absence of competing flora during antibiotic treatment.
Streptococcus pyogenes	Commonly introduced to hospitals by patients with strep-throat, certain strains invade the bloodstream and produce deadly toxins.
Clostridum difficile	Part of normal human gut flora, successful in absence of competing flora during antibiotic treatment, spore form resistant to environmental degradation, sterilization.

Unfortunately, the selection of antibiotics available to doctors remains essentially the same as it was ten years ago, even though antibiotic resistance is increasing at an alarming rate. In the past, doctors treated most infections with penicillin and reserved other antibiotics only for the rare instances where penicillin was ineffective. Now, penicillin is only effective against a handful of microorganisms. Without new antimicrobial drugs, the ultimate endpoint of increasing antibiotic resistance will be an increase in the number of deaths from infections, with hospital-acquired infections the most likely to be resistant to treatment. There is no end in sight for the problem of antibiotic resistance among microorganisms. Antibiotic discovery efforts are leveling off at drug companies, and fewer safe antibiotics are being discovered per year.

The increasing proportion of immunocompromised patients is another obstacle to infection control in hospitals. The number of immunocompromised people in the United States has risen throughout the last few decades because of increased longevity, AIDS, cancer chemotherapy, and organ transplantation procedures. This has created a hospital population that is not only susceptible to infection by classical pathogens, like *Salmonella*, but also to a variety of opportunistic pathogens, including *Pseudomonas aeruginosa* and *Staphylococcus aureus*. Immunocompromised patients in hospitals are especially challenging because they serve as reservoirs of opportunistic pathogens in addition to potential victims.

Hospital-acquired infections cannot be eliminated but can be reduced significantly by diligent infection control measures. The best way to control infections in hospitals is through sterilization of surgical instruments limited use of indwelling medical devices, routine disinfection of hands and surfaces, diligent wound care, and careful food preparation. Autoclaves are used in hospitals to sterilize heat-tolerant surgical instruments and other devices, but cannot be used in all situations. When autoclaves cannot be used, disinfectant chemicals are used to inactivate microorganisms on hands and surfaces in hospitals. One of the major benefits of routine disinfection is a reduction in the overall pathogen load in hospitals. Diligent wound care is also important because open wounds provide precisely the environment bacteria need to grow, thus wounds are very common sites of infection. Antiseptics and antibiotics applied to skin help reduce the burden of wound diseases. Hospital food can also be prepared carefully to prevent foodborne disease. For some highly susceptible individuals, food may even be sterilized to kill germs completely before it is served.

In the future, hospital-acquired infections are likely to be mitigated by novel antimicrobial technologies and innovative, non-invasive surgical procedures. Some novel antimicrobial technologies are already reducing the incidence of hospital-acquired infections. For example, catheters, which are left in the body for long periods of time, are the most common source of infections in hospitals. When coated with ionic silver, these devices inhibit the growth of bacteria and can reduce rates of infection by up to 50 percent. Non-invasive medical procedures also have the potential to reduce the number of hospital-acquired infections. For example, some cancers can now be treated with target-specific drugs, which are extremely effective and reduce the need for surgery. In the future, innovative medical procedures and antimicrobial technologies will help to prevent hospital-acquired infections and reduce dependence on antibiotics.

A great deal of litigation stems from hospital-acquired infections. However, deciding which cases have merit is challenging. In some cases, hospital-acquired infections are predictable side effects of more important medical treatments. In others, hospital-acquired infections are the direct result of negligence by hospital staff. In the worst cases, lethal infections are transmitted in hospitals to patients undergoing routine or minor treatment. A central part of most cases involving hospital-acquired infections is showing the ultimate source of the infection. For example, in 1998, a series of bloodstream infections at a hospital were caused by the bacterium *Serratia marcescens*, which was repeatedly isolated from the blood of several patients. Investigators learned through an epidemiological analysis that a respiratory therapy supervisor was tampering with hanging intravenous drug delivery systems to steal the potent narcotic Fentanyl. By doing so, she unwittingly contaminated many of the bags with fecal bacteria on her hands, resulting in at least nineteen severe infections (Jarvis 2003). By understanding disease transmission in hospitals, lawyers and judges will be able to navigate the nuances of hospital-acquired disease litigation and build and examine cases effectively.

11.3 Types of Hospital-Acquired Infections

Pathogens in hospitals can be transmitted to patients through many different routes. As Table 11.2 shows, the vast majority of hospital-acquired infections occur in one of five areas of the body. These are the urinary tract, lungs, bloodstream, gastrointestinal tract, and in tissue wounds. Thus, a useful way to consider hospital-acquired infections is by their location in the body, under the assumption that each part of the body is subject to similar medical procedures and therefore, similar exposures to microorganisms.

Table 11.2
Common Sites of Hospital-acquired Infections

Infection Site	Relevant Pathogens	Possible Cause
Urinary Tract	Uropathogenic *E. coli*, *Enterococcus*, *Pseudomonas aeruginosa*, *Candida albicans*, *Klebsiella pneumonia*	Use of indwelling urinary catheter, unhygienic care.
Wound	*Staphylococcus aureus*, Other *Staphylococcus* species, *Enterococcus*, *Pseudomonas aeruginosa*, *Enterobacter*	Bacteria from wounding object, environmental bacteria growing in wound, poor wound care or necrotic flesh.
Lungs	*Staphylococcus aureus*, *Pseudomonas aeruginosa*, *Enterobacter*, *Klebsiella pneumoniae*, *Legionella pneumophila*	Insertion of breathing tube, aspiration of food, inhalation of contaminated water droplets.
Gastrointestinal Tract	*E. coli*, *Salmonella*, *Enterococcus*, *Staphylococcus aureus*, *Clostridium difficile*	Ingestion of contaminated food, ingestion of contaminated water, reduction in normal flora by antibiotics.
Bloodstream	*Staphylococcus aureus*, Other *Staphylococcus* species, *Enterococcus*, *Pseudomonas aeruginosa*	Surgery, contaminated indwelling medical device, open wound, damaged internal organs.

A. Urinary Tract Infections

Urinary tract infections are common in the general public and are especially problematic in hospitals (Filetoth 2003). Urinary tract infections can be caused by sexually transmitted pathogens or by pathogens that enter the urethra through fecal contamination. Urinary tract infections in hospitals are almost always a result of fecal contamination.

Urinary catheters are by far the most significant risk factor for urinary tract infections in hospitals. Urinary catheters are a problem for three main reasons. First, catheters can transport bacteria from the environment or urethral opening to deep within the urethra during insertion. Second, some bacteria actually grow on the surface of catheters, providing a constant dose to the lining of the urethra. Lastly, certain types of urinary catheters, such as Foley catheters, remain in continuous contact with the delicate lining of the urethra, resulting in cuts or abrasions to the tissue and weakening the body's innate defenses against microorganisms.

Urinary tract infections are easy to detect. They should be suspected when a patient complains of increased frequency of urination, fever, or urinary pain. Infection is confirmed by microbiological analysis of urine or the presence of pus. Urine normally contains a low concentration of bacteria, which enter flowing urine as it passes over the urethral opening. Infected urinary tracts, however, excrete much greater numbers of bacteria. As a general rule, urine containing greater than 100,000 bacteria per milliliter signals an infection. Urinary tract infections tend to be more severe in women because microorganisms can more easily travel the short distance through the urethra to the bladder and kidneys. Once a patient has been diagnosed with a urinary tract infection, antibiotics can usually control the infection before it spreads to the bladder or kidneys.

B. Wound Infections

Wounds are a common infection site and provide near-perfect conditions for bacteria to grow. Wounds are warm, wet, and nutritive. The majority of wounds in hospitals are caused intentionally by needlesticks, incisions, and other procedures that break skin or tissue and leave it temporarily damaged. The number of punctures from sutures combined with incisions from scalpels can total in the hundreds for major surgeries. Other wounds are caused outside of the hospital, such as burn wounds or wounds from trauma.

The only thing that naturally protects wounds from bacteria is the immune system. Unfortunately, certain types of wounds are challenging for the immune system to defend. Infections are especially common in wounds with large surface area and high levels of exposure to environmental bacteria. In burn wounds, for example, the large surface area strains immune system resources while constant exposure to environmental bacteria provides numerous opportunities for infection. Wounds in areas that receive poor circulation also limit the ability of the immune system to control infections.

There are some generally accepted risk factors for wound infections. The first is the number of microorganisms that the wound is subjected to at the time it is inflicted. For medical procedures, this is largely a function of the level of contamination of the hospital environment and instruments, but may also be a function of a surgeon's skill level or ability to operate without damaging excess tissue. Although needles and scalpels are almost always sterile before use, microorganisms from the skin and other reservoirs, such as the intestines, contaminate them during use. During certain surgeries, intestinal spillage or other events might occur which introduce great numbers of microorganisms into wounds. For accidental wounds, the initial inoculum of microorganisms may come from the wounding object itself. For example, a deep splinter may carry thousands of soil-borne pathogens with it into the wound channel. Bullets and other objects may also drive bacteria from the body into wounds at the time that they are inflicted. Lack of circulation, lack of oxygen, and burn wounds also increase the likelihood of wound infection. Wounds that do not receive sufficient blood circulation are limited in terms of the number of immune cells that can travel to the wound to fight off infection. Lack of oxygen in a wound can also facilitate the growth of highly pathogenic anaerobic bacteria including *Clostridium tetani*, the cause of lockjaw, and *Clostridium perfringens*, the cause of gangrene. The length of time a wound is open is another risk factor for infection. Lengthy or exploratory surgeries may increase the likelihood of infection. The last major risk factor is the level of wound care. Great care should be taken to prevent wounds from coming into contact with microorganisms and to prevent further growth of microorganisms already in the wound. Wound care can include covering the wound, treating it with topical antibiotics, draining pus, and using systemic antibiotics. Under the best circumstances, the efficacy of the chosen antimicrobial agent can be verified by testing bacteria cultured from the wound for susceptibility to the drug in a laboratory.

Because of their ubiquitous nature, microorganisms can be cultured from most wounds at some point, but that does not necessarily indicate that wounds are seriously infected. In fact, some signs of infection are generally regarded as normal parts of wound healing, such as pain, redness, and swelling. Useful indicators of abnormal or serious wound infections are large amounts of pus in a wound, fever, or bacteria in the bloodstream. Large amounts of pus indicate that a major immune reaction is occurring in the wound. Fever from a wound may also indicate the same thing, or may indicate that an infection has entered the bloodstream. Bacteremia or sepsis, as detected by blood culture, is a sure sign of a serious infection.

C. Pneumonia

Pneumonia can be caused by lung infections and is a common hospital-acquired disease. Infectious pneumonia is caused either by pathogens from the community or by pathogens specific to hospitals. Community-acquired pneumonia (CAP) arises in hospitals as a result of depression of the immune system due to another illness. Pneumonia of this type usually occurs within 5 days of admission to a hospital and is caused by a small but distinctive set of microorganisms, including several species of *Pneumococcus*, *Mycoplasma*, *Haemophilius*, *Branchamella*, *Staphylococcus*, *Klebsiella*, *Legionella*, and a few viruses. Hospital-acquired pneumonia (HAP) usually arises later, and is caused by agitation of respiratory tissues by medical devices like respirators or bacteria prevalent in the hospital environment, including several species of *Pseudomonas*, *Acinetobacter*, *Bacteriodes*, and enteric bacteria (Filetoth 2003).

Important risk factors for hospital-acquired pneumonia are the overall presence of respiratory pathogens in the hospital environment, the amount of agitation of respiratory tissue, and inhalation of food or liquid, called aspiration. The load of respiratory pathogens in a hospital depends on the quality of air handling systems, the degree to which patients with respiratory illness are separated from patients with good respiratory health and the general cleanliness of the hospital environment. Invasive measures such as mechanical respiration lower immune defenses in airways. Accidental inhalation of food and water, called aspiration, is also a risk factor for pneumonia. If microbially contaminated food or water repeatedly enters the lungs, it may promote growth of bacteria. Special care should be given to individuals who are unconscious or have swallowing disorders to mitigate this risk.

The ultimate source of pneumonia in a hospital patient may be difficult to identify because of the multiple exposures to microorganisms our lungs receive on a daily basis. There are some exceptions, such as when *Legionella* is spread through a contaminated air conditioning system or a patient develops pneumonia as a result of aspiration, but proving a clear cause of acquired pneumonia from a hospital is rare.

D. Gastrointestinal infections

Gastrointestinal infections in hospitals are problematic because they introduce billions of infectious agents into the hospital, they are highly transmissible, and they can be deadly to high-risk patients. Gastrointestinal infections can be initiated by as few as one infectious microorganism. This is especially problematic in hospitals, where gastrointestinal pathogens have the opportunity to infect other parts of the body, including the blood, urinary tract, lungs, and wounds.

Major risk factors for gastrointestinal disease in hospitals are immunological status of the patient, cleanliness of hospital surfaces (including hands), consumption of improperly prepared or handled food, and the use of antibiotics. The immunological status of a patient is especially important because it is often highly correlated to the severity of gastrointestinal disease. For example, if someone with a healthy immune system were to become infected by the parasite *Cryptosporidium parvum*, they would probably have watery diarrhea for between one and three weeks, whereas a late-stage AIDS patient may develop other symptoms and may never clear the infection. One of the most significant risk factors for gastrointestinal disease in hospitals is the use of antibiotics. The intestines are colonized by trillions of non-pathogenic microorganisms, which compete against pathogens for space and nutrients within the intestines. When an antibiotic is administered, it spreads throughout the body and many of these protective microbes are killed. This can create advantageous circumstances for pathogenic microorganisms, especially those that have even minor resistance to antibiotics. During antibiotic treatment, such pathogens proliferate and cause infection. The pathogenic bacterium most commonly responsible for this type of infection is *Clostridium difficile*, an environmentally resistant spore-forming bacterium that causes diarrhea. The microbiological cleanliness of surfaces and hands is another risk factor for gastrointestinal diseases in hospitals, because gastrointestinal pathogens can be spread indirectly from fecal matter to the mouth. Surfaces can act as intermediary reservoirs. Exposure to gastrointestinal pathogens can be minimized by regularly disinfecting potential carriers of microorganisms including hands and inanimate objects. Finally, consumption of contaminated food may put patients at risk for gastrointestinal disease. Foodborne diseases are a problem in hospitals because a large amount of food is prepared, many immunocompromised people are served, and a significant amount of food handling is required to deliver and serve food to patients. Like any other facility, hospitals should take precautions to prevent the spread of pathogens through food. Food should be kept frozen or refrigerated until just before it is cooked, cooked thoroughly, and then served or refrigerated immediately. Food delivered to patients should be maintained at proper temperatures or should be delivered immediately after cooking. Handling of food by hospital employees should be minimized.

Whether or not a gastrointestinal infection is treatable with drugs depends on the type of microorganism causing the infection. Stool specimens can be analyzed to determine the causative agent of diarrhea. In some cases, no agent will be identified in stool, and doctors must make their diagnosis based on symptoms alone. If a virus is found, antibiotics will not help, and the diarrhea must simply be managed until the body can clear the infection. If bacteria or parasites are causing the infection, antibiotics may help, but they should be used with care to avoid causing antibiotic-associated diarrhea.

E. Bloodstream infections

Bacteria and bacterial toxins in the bloodstream can be lethal and are a major problem in hospitals. The condition of having bacteria in the bloodstream is referred to as sepsis, septicemia, bacteremia, or microbemia. Some bloodstream infections are transient and may go completely undetected. These infections are usually referred to as bacteremia or microbemia. Bacteremia can sometimes be detected after brushing or flossing teeth or after someone is wounded. Most of the time, bacteria are naturally and quickly removed by the immune system and a sample of blood taken a few hours after the event will be sterile. Infections of the blood are called sepsis. Sepsis is caused by bacteria growing or secreting toxins in the bloodstream. Recurrent bacteremia without an assignable cause indicates that sepsis may eventually occur in a patient. A bloodstream infection is different from a bloodborne infection, in that the infecting microorganism actually grows or produces toxins in the blood rather than just traveling through the blood to get to its normal site of infection.

There are two main causes of sepsis. The first, called a primary bloodstream infection, occurs when bacteria enter the bloodstream from an outside source (such as a contaminated needle) and grow in the bloodstream. This type of infection is rare in hospitals. Secondary bloodstream infections are much more common in hospitals. During secondary bloodstream infections, microorganisms grow in some part of the body and are constantly or intermittently spilled into the bloodstream. Sources of microorganisms in the body may include infected wounds, ruptured organs, and indwelling medical devices. In order to reduce the risk of secondary bloodstream infections, wounds should be cared for diligently and indwelling medical devices should be sterile during implantation and maintained as needed to prevent the growth of bacteria.

Signs of bacteremia include fever, general malaise, and weakness. Signs of sepsis include high fever, vomiting, diarrhea, and lowered blood pressure. Because sepsis can be deadly, antibiotics should be used immediately to control the infection. If a bloodstream infection is transitory or mild, samples of blood can be cultured before treatment to identify the most appropriate antibiotic and to help doctors to identify the internal source of the infection if it has not been previously determined.

11.4 Handwashing, Disinfection, and Sterilization

In contrast to schools, restaurants, and other facilities where disinfection is routine, hospitals accommodate many people who are actively infected with growing, reproducing pathogens. This makes the risk of infectious disease transmission much higher. While administering care, doctors, nurses, and other staff can transmit pathogenic microorganisms between patients, hands, and objects. Potential pathogen carriers include surgical instruments, hands, laundry, food, hard surfaces, air, water, furniture, and small objects like cellular phones. Thus, inactivating microorganisms in the hospital environment is crucial to controlling the spread of infectious disease.

Sterilization of surgical instruments and other medical devices is the most important way to prevent the spread of infectious diseases in hospitals. Medical objects can be sterilized in two ways. The first and most common way is to use an autoclave. Autoclaves are like large ovens that are pressurized with steam to increase heat transfer to objects and prevent liquids from boiling. A typical autoclave subjects an object to high pressure and a temperature of 100°C for twenty to thirty minutes. If optimal temperatures and pressures are achieved, autoclaves completely inactivate all microorganisms relevant to human health except for prions, which are only inactivated by high temperatures and certain acidic or oxidative liquids. The second way that objects and devices are sterilized in hospitals is through immersion in potent disinfectant solutions for extended periods of time. This is called chemical sterilization and is common for instruments that are large or sensitive to heat, such as surgical endoscopes. Glutaraldehyde is one example of a sterilant chemical. Unfortunately, sterilant chemicals are dangerous to handle and can have difficulty penetrating and sterilizing porous surfaces. The Food and Drug Administration (FDA) oversees certification of sterilant chemicals and verifies their efficacy.

Disinfectants and germicides, which are two different names for the same thing, are different than sterilant chemicals. Disinfectants and germicides are used to inactivate pathogens on non-surgical objects and devices in hospitals, whereas sterilant chemicals are used to sterilize medical devices prior to use. Disinfectants are generally milder than sterilants. Disinfectants play a major role in preventing transmission of pathogens between objects and people in hospitals. For example, treatment of hospital laundry with bleach as a disinfectant helps to assure that pathogens from one patient do not come into contact with the next.

Disinfectants are considered by the USEPA to be pesticides and are regulated by the Federal Insecticide, Fungicide, and Rodenticide Act (FIFRA). For a product to be marketed as a disinfectant, it must be certified by the USEPA to have passed specific laboratory tests that verify the chemical's ability to kill certain classes of microorganisms. These tests are carried out according to product label instructions. Therefore it is crucial that hospital disinfectants are used in accordance with label instructions to ensure that the disinfectant is working properly. Disinfectants must also demonstrate chemical stability after they are manufactured. In general, a disinfectant that still works after one year of storage is considered to be acceptable. Disinfectants must meet special requirements to be considered "industrial-grade" or "hospital-strength." Specifically, these chemicals must have demonstrated high-level antimicrobial efficacy against the following microorganisms under label instructions: *Staphylococcus aureus*, *Salmonella choleraesuis*, and *Pseudomonas aeruginosa*. The requirement for activity against *Pseudomonas aeruginosa* sets hospital-grade disinfectants apart from those intended for use in the home. Since *Pseudomonas aeruginosa* is a significant cause of hospital-acquired infections, it is not appropriate to use disinfectants in hospitals that do not indicate on the label that they are effective against this microorganism. Bleach and solutions containing quaternary ammonium compounds (quats) are the chemicals most frequently used to disinfect hospitals.

Handwashing and the use of hand sanitizers are other ways to reduce the spread of microorganisms to patients in hospitals. Thorough handwashing with plain soap and water removes 90 percent or more of microorganisms on hands. Antimicrobial chemicals are added to some hand soaps to kill remaining microorganisms. However, care should be exercised in hospitals because the FDA has expressed concern that the levels of antimicrobial agents in hand soap are too low to have any real impact on infectious disease transmission. In addition, a common antimicrobial additive in soap, Triclosan, has been linked to the development of antibiotic resistance in laboratory microorganisms, although antibiotic resistance as a result of Triclosan use has not yet been observed in practice (Russell 2003). Alcohol-based hand sanitizers can also be used to reduce the number of microorganisms on hands and prevent the spread of microorganisms in hospitals. Hand sanitizers are chemicals that are certified to kill at least 99 percent of bacteria on hands. The FDA regulates hand sanitizers, which are typically inexpensive and easy to use.

Microbiologists sometimes refer to a general hierarchy of resistance to biocides, wherein prions are the microorganisms most resistant to disinfectants, followed by spore-forming bacteria, parasitic cysts, unenveloped viruses, fungi, bacteria, and finally enveloped viruses, which are most sensitive to disinfectants. However, the arrangement of microorganisms with respect to their resistance to disinfectants can change depending on the biocide and microorganism. For example, *Cryptosporidium parvum* is highly resistant to chlorine, but is sensitive to ultraviolet light. In contrast, adenoviruses are resistant to ultraviolet light but are sensitive to chlorine. Therefore, lawyers and judges should not assume that a chemical capable of disinfecting a "more resistant" microorganism would necessarily kill one that is believed to be more sensitive in the absence of confirmatory data.

11.5 Commonly Implicated Pathogens

Staphylococcus aureus

Staphylococcus aureus is a gram-positive, spherically shaped bacterium that is notably resistant to drying and is a normal part of human skin flora. Certain strains of *Staphylococcus aureus* have increased virulence and marked resistance to a broad spectrum of antibiotics. If a clinical isolate of *Staphylococcus aureus* is tested for resistance to antibiotics including methicillin and is susceptible only to the highest-level drugs, like Vancomycin, it is called methicillin-resistant *Staphylococcus aureus* (MRSA). Although *Staphylococcus* rarely invades tissue on its own, it is a successful opportunist and can grow if it is allowed inside. When growing in the body, *Staphylococcus aureus* can produce potent exotoxins. If large quantities are produced, fever, dangerously low blood pressure, and even death may result.

Staphylococcus aureus is a common cause of hospital-acquired infections and MRSA infections are increasing at an alarming rate. It is the most common cause of surgical wound infections and pneumonia, and the second most common cause of blood infections (Brock 2000). In addition, *Staphylococcus aureus* spreads in many ways, including through contaminated medical devices and other inanimate objects, person-to-person contact, and food. Infections with this bacterium are common after surgery or implantation of medical devices. Tissue and blood infections with *Staphylococcus aureus* are particularly risky because certain strains produce toxins that can cause toxic-shock syndrome and may lead to death. Over time, implanted devices may have to be removed to control infections with *Staphylococcus aureus*. Staphylococcal pneumonia is also a problem in hospitals. Presumably, *Staphylococcus aureus* infects the lungs after other infecting bacteria or respiratory viruses invade and damage tissues. *Staphylococcus aureus* can also cause gastrointestinal disease. Food poisoning by *Staphylococcus aureus* is very rarely associated with mortality. Usually, a person ingests a small amount of pre-formed toxin and falls ill between one and six hours later. Symptoms include vomiting, severe diarrhea, and nausea.

Staphylococcus aureus has succeeded as a hospital pathogen because of its "second life" as a normal component of human microbial flora. Microbiologists can detect this bacterium on the skin of around one in three people at any given time. Additionally, large numbers of this bacterium may be present in the intestines and upper respiratory tract. Being a normal part of human bacterial flora allows *Staphylococcus aureus* to adapt to antibiotics and to living in and around our bodies *before* humans try to fight it as an infection. Indeed, *Staphylococcus aureus* has been quick to acquire antibiotic resistance, as evidenced by multiple drug-resistant varieties such as MRSA. Most *Staphylococcus aureus* infections appear to be opportunistic in nature.

Streptococcus pyogenes

Streptococcus pyogenes is a gram-positive bacterium that is spherical in shape and is found in short linear arrangements, resembling beads on a string. Many members of the genus *Streptococcus* are part of normal human microbial flora. However, some species, especially *Streptococcus pyogenes*, are remarkably virulent.

Streptococcus pyogenes is the common cause of strep throat and also causes rare but severe necrotic tissue infections. Strep throat is rarely life threatening if treated immediately with antibiotics and is not regularly transmitted within hospitals. Without prompt antibiotic treatment, a small percentage of infected individuals will go on to develop rheumatic fever, which is an autoimmune disease that can lead to heart damage. The most serious hospital-acquired infections from *Streptococcus pyogenes* are "flesh-eating" infections. *Streptococcus pyogenes* does not actually eat flesh. Rather, in some systemic infections it invades subcutaneous tissue and produces potent toxins that damage tissue and cause a severe overreaction by the immune system. Such infections are lethal in up to 30 percent of patients (Brock 2000). Unlike many other pathogens, *Streptococci* remain susceptible to most first-generation antibiotics, including penicillin.

Pseudomonas aeruginosa

Pseudomonas aeruginosa is a Gram-negative, rod-shaped bacterium that is ubiquitous in the environment. It can be isolated from many places within hospitals, including drinking water, various foods (especially vegetables), the human body, and inanimate objects. *Pseudomonas aeruginosa* is naturally surrounded by a gelatinous coating that protects it from disinfectants and antibiotics.

Resistance to the environment, disinfectants, and antibiotics makes *Pseudomonas aeruginosa* a major source of hospital-acquired infections. It is the most frequent infection in burn patients, the second leading cause of hospital-acquired pneumonia, the third most common cause of hospital-acquired urinary tract infections, and the fourth leading cause of surgical wound infections (Maier 2000). *Pseudomonas aeruginosa* also poses a special risk to those with cystic fibrosis, where it can colonize the airway in a thick layer and is resistant to treatment with antibiotics. Prevention of *Pseudomonas aeruginosa* infections in hospitals depends on aseptic surgical techniques, diligent disinfection of hospital surfaces with hospital strength disinfectants, use of ethanol-based hand sanitizers, and careful care of burn wounds.

Candida albicans

Candida albicans is a fungus that exists in two forms in the human body. In normal individuals, it exists as a simple yeast, feeding on residual nutrients in the mouth and digestive tract. However, it can also transform into a pathogenic form, where it produces invasive hyphae that adhere strongly to human tissues. The result of this change is infection and colonization of susceptible tissues. Disease from *Candida albicans* is commonly manifested as vaginal yeast infections or oral thrush. *Candida albicans* is a unique agent of hospital-acquired infection because it is not a bacterium. It is a normal part of human microbial flora, but can become a problem if the immune system is weakened. Infections with *Candida albicans* are generally not life threatening. Infections of the mouth and vagina with *Candida albicans* are not likely to be a result of hospital disease transmission. Rather, patients bring the pathogen in with them as a normal component of their body flora (in its normal place in the body) and infections are activated during immunosuppression. If, however, this yeast is observed in the bloodstream or the lungs, it may be a hospital-acquired infection.

Vancomycin-resistant Enterococcus

Enterococcus is a gram-positive, spherical bacterium found in the intestines. It is related to both *Streptococcus* (another relevant hospital pathogen) and *Lactococcus* ("helpful" bacteria found in dairy products). Although normally sheltered by the moist environment inside the human body, *Enterococcus* can survive being dried on surfaces. The most clinically important member of the *Enterococcus* genus is *Enterococcus faecalis*.

Infections with *Enterococcus* have been spread through hospitals for some time. Between 1990 and 1996, *Enterococcus* wass the fourth most common hospital-acquired infection, responsible for 16 percent of all urinary tract infections, 12 percent of all surgical wound infections, 9 percent of all blood infections, and 2 percent of all pneumonia (Brock 2000). Recently, some strains of this microorganism, namely *Enterococcus faecalis*, have developed resistance to a wide range of antibiotics, including potent Vancomycin. The advent of antibiotic resistance in this common hospital-acquired pathogen is a major obstacle to treatment and an example of the specter of rising antibiotic resistance among bacteria in general.

Uropathogenic *E. coli*

Escherichia coli is a species of gram-negative, rod-shaped bacteria that is present in human intestines. Although the vast majority of *E. coli* is harmless, a few strains carry genes that enable them to spread effectively and produce severe disease in hospitals. One of the most clinically important strains is uropathogenic *E. coli*. This *E. coli* has special hair-like external structures that enable it to bind tightly to the lining of the urinary tract, decreasing the natural ability of the body to flush out urinary pathogens.

E. coli is a significant hospital pathogen, especially as the cause of urinary tract infections. It is probably the most common cause of urinary tract infections in hospital patients. Between 1990 and 1996, *E. coli* were responsible for approximately 24 percent of urinary tract infections where a causative agent could be identified. During the same period, *E. coli* caused 8 percent of all surgical wound infections, 5 percent of all blood infections, and 4 percent of all pneumonia (Brock 2000). Fortunately, *E. coli* has not yet shown the antibiotic resistance characteristic of other hospital-transmitted bacteria.

11.6 Chapter Summary

Hospital-acquired infections are major problem in hospitals and a source of litigation. A great deal of disease transmission occurs in hospitals because there is an abnormally high concentration of people with active infections, there is much close personal contact, and many people in hospitals have depressed immune systems. Handwashing and disinfection of inanimate objects in hospitals reduces the overall burden of infectious microorganisms and the risk of hospital-acquired infections. Infections transmitted in hospitals occur most frequently in the urinary tract, the bloodstream, the lungs, the gastrointestinal tract, and in wounds. Invasive treatments in hospitals facilitate the transmission of certain diseases. Many of the most significant hospital pathogens, including *Staphylococcus aureus*, *Enterococcus faecalis*, and *Pseudomonas aeruginosa*, show marked resistance to antibiotics, can be spread in many ways, and can infect many different parts of the body. Antibiotic resistance among human pathogens is more common in hospitals than anywhere else. Antibiotic use applies significant selective pressure to bacteria to acquire antibiotic resistance and the number of antibiotic resistant bacteria is increasing in hospitals.

Chapter 12

Biological Weapons

Synopsis

12.1 Chapter Preview

A number of microorganisms and toxins produced by microorganisms can be used as weapons. Biological weapons were researched and developed extensively during the Cold War by large governments, but now the biggest threat is that terrorists will use them. This chapter describes the pathogens that could be used as weapons, symptoms of disease, and the way that the diseases would spread if they were ever to be released deliberately. Lawyers, judges, and law enforcement personnel should be aware of intentional misuse of microorganisms, because biological weapons have been used at least twice in the United States already and their availability makes it likely that they will be used in the future.

12.2 Introduction

People have used biological weapons for nearly a millennium. The first recorded use of microorganisms as a weapon was in 1346, when Tartar forces besieging Kaffa catapulted the bodies of plague victims into the city to spread the disease and weaken the opposing army. Throughout the European expansion of the sixteenth century, microorganisms serving as weapons facilitated entire conquests. In some cases, conquistadors would return to the New World a decade after introducing European diseases like smallpox to find populations reduced by three-quarters or more.

During the twentieth century, nations researched and developed a handful of pathogens to make them more manufacturable, dispersible, and formidable as weapons. The United States, Russia, the United Kingdom, and other countries all supported intensive biological weapon development programs. Although the programs were highly secretive, some were exposed by deadly accidents. In 1942, the British tested an anthrax-releasing bomb on Gruinard Island in Scotland, making the land uninhabitable for decades. In 1979, anthrax spores were accidentally released from a weapon development facility in Sverdlovsk, Russia. Less than one gram of spores was released, but at least sixty-six people in the nearby countryside died of pulmonary Anthrax disease as a result. More recently, a biological weapon research facility in Frederick, Maryland had to be completely sealed following an inadvertent release of Anthrax. Some of the most chilling information about biological weapon development came to light from defecting Soviet scientists who testified that research at Soviet facilities during the Cold War was eerily advanced. According to ex-Soviet scientists, a whole range of biological weapons were engineered, including antibiotic-resistant anthrax and pathogens that would trick the immune system into attacking the body indefinitely after a mild initial infection with a microorganism. Biologically engineered pathogens were even tested in "real life" against monkeys tethered to poles to assess the damage that they could do to human populations.

Intensive biological weapon development by world superpowers shows that biological weapons are an attractive choice for conventional warfare, but biological weapons have an even greater appeal to terrorists and rogue governments because many are easy to acquire and invoke fear and uncertainty among those affected. Even medium-threat biological weapons could be highly disruptive under the right circumstances. For example, if someone working at a milk plant were to inoculate the finished product with even a moderately virulent gastrointestinal pathogen, like *Salmonella*, the resulting outbreak of disease could be devastating. More importantly to terrorists, the outbreak would surely make people feel less safe because microorganisms are difficult to see and understand. Although moderately virulent biological weapons are probably the easiest for terrorists to obtain and use, highly virulent pathogens represent the biggest threat. For this reason, biological weapons are referred to as the "poor man's atomic bomb." For example, a suicidal terrorist infected with smallpox virus could travel to crowded "target" areas and cause inestimable death, chaos and misery.

Biological agents have been used against domestic targets by terrorists at least twice in the United States. In 1984, members of a religious group called the Rajneeshees contaminated salad bars at restaurants in The Dalles, Oregon, in an attempt to influence local elections. They obtained *Salmonella typhimurium* from a nurse working at a local hospital and intentionally used it to contaminate ten salad bars. In all, 751 people developed Salmonellosis (Brock 2000). Fortunately, no one died. The second domestic attack occurred in 2001 and involved weapons-grade *Bacillus anthracis* sent in envelopes through the mail to politicians and news agencies. The attacks occurred over a period of several weeks, a week after terrorists used hijacked planes to destroy the Twin Towers in New York City. In all, it is thought that seven letters containing *Bacillus anthracis* were mailed. Intended recipients included Senators Tom Daschle and Patrick Leahy, and various people at the news organizations NBC, CBS, and ABC in New York, and AMI in Florida (See Figures 12.1 and 12.2). Ultimately, twenty-two people contracted anthrax and five people died as a result, including two mail facility employees and three others who are suspected to have been infected as a result of cross-contamination of mail. In the first wave of attacks, the anthrax was described as a low-grade, chunky material resembling ground dog food. In the second wave of attacks, which targeted only the senators, anthrax contained in the envelopes was refined, having the consistency of talcum powder. Later, it was learned that all of the anthrax used in the attacks was from the same strain, called the Ames strain, which was developed as a biological weapon by the United States. The high grade of the weapon used, along with the inherent risk of handling it, strongly suggests that someone with a high level of microbiological expertise carried out the attacks. No one has yet been charged with committing the attacks, although thousands of subpoenas have been issued and thousands of people have been interviewed about their potential involvement.

Figure 12.1 *Letter sent to Senator Daschle containing Anthrax.*

Figure 12.2 *Letter sent to Senator Leahy containing Anthrax.*

There are benefits and drawbacks associated with using microorganisms as weapons. Some benefits are that biological weapons can be lethal or incapacitating, they are relatively inexpensive and easy to make, they can be obtained and cultivated from natural sources, and they can be deployed secretly. On the other hand, many biological weapons kill indiscriminately, are difficult to disseminate, and require at least a collegiate understanding of microbiology to handle safely.

The United States government divides pathogens into categories according to their potential for use as weapons. (See Table 12.1) Category A biological weapons are a select group of pathogens with a high potential to cause adverse public health affects on a large scale. Category A biological weapons include *Bacillus anthracis*, smallpox virus, botulinum toxin (derived from the bacterium *Clostridium botulinum*), *Yersinia pestis* (the cause of plague), *Tularemia* (the cause of rabbit fever), and hemorrhagic viruses including Ebola and Marburg viruses. Each of these microorganisms has special characteristics that give it the ability to cause great harm. Spores of *Bacillus anthrac*is are remarkably resistant to environmental degradation and chemical disinfectants, and infection causes death in nearly all untreated pulmonary cases. Smallpox virus is highly communicable and most people have no immunity against the disease since vaccination ceased after its eradication in 1979. The bacterium that causes the plague, *Yersinia pestis*, is communicable by aerosols and is highly lethal. *Tularemia* is an easily spread bacterial infection that results in incapacitating fever, pneumonia, and headaches. Hemorrhagic viruses can be spread from person to person and are rapidly lethal in up to 90 percent of cases. Category B agents have less potential as weapons but could still cause great harm if used knowledgeably. There are many Category B agents, including *Brucella* (the cause of brucellosis), Burkholderia mallei (the cause of Glanders), *Coxiella burnetti* (the cause of Q Fever), *Rickettsia prowazekii* (the cause of Typhus), encephalitis viruses, enteric bacteria that could be used against the food supply, and some bacterially derived toxins. Category C agents also exist, but have much less potential for use as weapons. For example, *Mycobacterium* tuberculosis is a category C agent. Although it causes a serious disease, it is extremely difficult to grow in a laboratory and is difficult to spread.

Safety precautions that should be taken in the event that a biological weapon is used depend on the unique characteristics of the pathogen. In the event that the pathogen was highly communicable through air, precautions should be taken to isolate infected individuals and filter the air breathed through small-particle trapping filters. Public areas and crowds, as well as potentially contaminated inanimate objects, should be avoided. If the pathogen was inoculated into food or water, these items should be boiled or cooked thoroughly before being eaten. In the event that toxins are introduced into food or water, these items should be avoided until the extent of contamination is clear.

Table 12.1
Microorganisms That Could be Used as Weapons

Biological Agent	Type	Disease	Threat Level
Bacillus anthracis	Bacterium	Anthrax	A
Francisella tularensis	Bacterium	Rabbit fever	A
Yersinia pestis	Bacterium	Pneumonic Plague	A
Botulinum toxin	Toxin	Botulism	A
Ebola virus	Virus	Hemorrhagic fever	A
Marburg virus	Virus	Hemorrhagic fever	A
Smallpox virus	Virus	Smallpox	A
Brucella abortus	Bacterium	Brucellosis	B
Burkholderia pseudomallei	Bacterium	Melioidosis	B
Coxiella burnetii	Bacterium	Q Fever	B
E. coli O157:H7	Bacterium	Severe Diarrhea	B
Rickettsia prowazekii	Bacterium	Typhus	B
Salmonella	Bacterium	Salmonellosis	B
Shigella	Bacterium	Diarrhea	B
Vibrio cholerae	Bacterium	Diarrhea	B
Cryptosporidium	Parasite	Diarrhea	B
Staphylococcal enterotoxin B	Toxin	Diarrhea, Shock	B
Alphavirus	Virus	Encephalitis	B
Equine Encephalitis virus	Virus	Encephalitis	B
Hepatitis A virus	Virus	Hepatitis	B
Mycobacterium tuberculosis	Bacterium	Tuberculosis	C
Giardia	Parasite	Diarrhea	C
HIV	Virus	AIDS	C
Influenza virus	Virus	Influenza	C
Norovirus	Virus	Diarrhea	C

Judges and lawyers should be aware of the threat posed by the intentional use of microorganisms to cause harm. Biological weapons have been used domestically at least twice to date, and there is a chance that some outbreaks that have been attributed to "natural" sources were caused intentionally. Attorneys also play a special role in defining bioterrorism where its definition is murky. For example, is a sick fast-food worker who intentionally coughs on customers' hamburgers to make them sick a bioterrorist? The availability of many medium and low-threat biological agents make intentionally caused outbreaks a near certainty in the future. Attorneys can prepare themselves for such cases by learning about intentional transmission of infectious diseases.

12.3 Bacteria of Concern

Bacillus anthracis

Bacillus anthracis is the name of the bacterium that causes Anthrax. It is a gram-positive, rod-shaped bacterium that is relatively large. It is able to grow rapidly and has relatively simple nutritional requirements. In nature, *Bacillus anthracis* is spread to herbivores through a unique disease transmission cycle. An herbivore is first infected by *Bacillus anthracis* in the lungs, where bacteria grow rapidly and spread to the bloodstream, eventually killing it. As the host decomposes, the *Bacillus anthracis* transform from fast-growing bacteria into hardy spores, eventually depositing on the ground where the animal's corpse degraded. The spores reside there for years until the next grazer comes along and inhales them, initiating the cycle of infection once more.

There are three types of anthrax infections in humans. Skin contact with *Bacillus anthracis* produces a disease called cutaneous anthrax. Cutaneous anthrax consists of a small, dark ulcer that gradually grows larger. Interestingly, the skin ulcers produced by *Bacillus anthracis* are normally painless. If treated, cutaneous anthrax is rarely fatal. *Bacillus anthracis* can also infect the gastrointestinal tract. Gastrointestinal anthrax infections produce diarrhea and bloody vomit. If left untreated, gastrointestinal anthrax infections can be fatal. The last, and most serious form of disease produced by *Bacillus anthracis* is pulmonary anthrax, where inhaled spores lodge in the lungs and reproduce rapidly. The bacteria eventually spread into the bloodstream, completely overwhelming the immune system. Without antibiotic treatment, pulmonary anthrax is fatal in nearly all cases. Pulmonary anthrax can be treated with antibiotics, but treatment must start before or just after the onset of symptoms to be effective.

Bacillus anthracis is a key potential biological weapon because it is environmentally resistant, is easily transmitted through aerosols, and is not likely to produce epidemic disease. In spore form, *Bacillus anthracis* can lie dormant for decades yet remain infective. In addition, it is extremely resistant to disinfectants. In practice, only a few chemicals are capable of killing *Bacillus anthracis* spores, most of which are hazardous. In nature, *Bacillus anthracis* particles are found in large clumps, which limits the distance they can travel through aerosols. However, weaponized anthrax, which has been specially treated to separate spore clusters, can travel much greater distances and the smaller particles are more likely to lodge deep within lung tissues. *Bacillus anthracis* is one of the few pathogens spread by air that does not display person-to-person secondary transmission. This means that attacks can target specific groups while sparing the rest of the human population.

Francisella tularensis

Francisella tularensis is the name of the bacterium that causes Tularensis or Rabbit Fever. It is a small, gram-negative, rod-shaped microorganism that grows preferentially in the presence of oxygen. Insects associated with rabbits spread this microorganism in nature, but it can be spread deliberately through aerosols. Doses of as few as thirty are thought to cause disease in humans through air. *Francisella* can affect the body in many different ways, resulting in different diseases. In some cases, the bacterium infects the lungs predominantly and disease is severe. In others, lymph nodes are the major site of infection and fever may be the major symptom of infection.

Tularensis has an incubation period from three days to two weeks. Disease is characterized a persistent and incapacitating high fever that can last for many weeks. Person-to-person spread of *Francisella tularensis* has not been observed. *Tularensis* can be treated with antibiotics.

Francisella tularensis could be used as a biological weapon for many reasons. Like *Bacillus anthracis*, it is spread by aerosols and does not demonstrate a great deal of secondary transmission. Unlike *Bacillus anthracis*, however, *Francisella tularensis* infection is not normally fatal. Thus, the bacterium could be used to incapacitate people. If used as a biological weapon, *Francicella tularensis* would be likely to produce punctuated, confined outbreaks of disease. Francicella tularensis is susceptible to environmental degradation, chemical disinfectants, and antibiotics.

Yersinia pestis

Yersinia pestis is the name of the bacterium that causes both bubonic and pneumonic plague. It is a gram-negative, rod shaped microorganism that is most commonly spread by the bite of an infected tick associated with rodents. *Yersinia pestis* can also be spread from person to person through air. Once it is in the bloodstream, it replicates too quickly for the immune system to control.

Yersinia pestis produces two kinds of disease, depending on the mode of transmission. If the bacterium is introduced to the body from the bite of a flea, bubonic plague will develop. During bubonic plague, *Yersinia pestis* from the flea travels to lymph nodes and begins to multiply. Proliferation in the lymph nodes leads to severe swelling. The swollen lymph nodes are referred to as buboes. Eventually, bacteria spill into the bloodstream causing sepsis. Death from bubonic plague usually happens within five days of infection. The second form of the plague is known as pneumonic plague and occurs when people inhale *Yersinia pestis*. During pneumonic plague, *Yersinia pestis* multiplies in the lungs and then spills into the bloodstream. This form of the disease usually results in death within two days and can easily be transmitted to other people. Occasionally, people with bubonic plague will develop the pneumonic form of the disease. Antibiotic treatment of plague is only effective before or just after the onset of symptoms.

Yersinia pestis is a powerful but indiscriminant biological weapon because it can be spread easily from person to person in the pneumonic form. Fortunately, this bacterium is susceptible to environmental degradation and is sensitive to most disinfectants. A vaccine is available that can prevent this disease, but it does help someone who is already infected.

Brucella abortus

Brucella abortus is a gram-negative, elliptically shaped bacterium that only grows in the presence of oxygen. *Brucella abortus* was so named because it causes spontaneous abortions in cattle. *Brucella abortus* is the most common cause of brucellosis in humans, but a few other species can also cause the disease, including *Brucella suis, melitensis*, and *canis*. *Brucella* grows in livestock and normally infects animal handlers through abrasions in the skin. It can also be transmitted through aerosols. After infection, the microorganism establishes a persistent infection and can change its appearance to the immune system when under immune pressure. In the United States, brucellosis is sometimes spread through contaminated dairy products.

Brucellosis can be either acute or chronic. Acute brucellosis is characterized by high fever, chills and sweating for a period of up to eight weeks. Chronic, or undulant brucellosis is similar to the acute form of the disease, but fevers subside and recur many times over an extended period of time, up to one year. Chronic Brucellosis can also result in arthritis and inflammation of the heart.

Brucella abortus has many characteristics that make it a potential biological weapon. First, it can be spread through aerosols, making distribution among large populations possible. The bacterium also produces a disease that is typically non-lethal, but lasts for weeks or months in an infected person. In addition, the bacterium can be isolated from cattle, which are readily accessible. Person to person spread is not common, which means there is a low probability of an epidemic resulting from its use as a weapon. Brucellosis can be treated with the antibiotics streptomycin or erythromycin.

Enteric bacterial pathogens

With a few exceptions, enteric bacterial pathogens are gram-negative and rod-shaped, and can grow either with or without oxygen. Enteric bacterial pathogens include *Campylobacter, Shigella, E. coli, Clostridium difficile,* and *Vibrio cholerae*. These bacteria cause disease by producing toxins that harm the gastrointestinal tract. During an infection, enteric bacterial pathogens are excreted in great numbers in the feces of an infected person, but infections are normally cleared by the immune system within two weeks.

High doses of *Salmonella, Shigella, E. coli, Vibrio cholerae,* and *Campylobacter* cause profuse diarrhea and nausea, and may lead to lethal dehydration and kidney damage. During infection, billions of bacterial progeny are expelled from the body, which can lead to secondary transmission of disease and contamination of inanimate objects.

Enteric bacteria have the potential to be used as biological weapons. *Salmonella* already has been used as such in the United States. There are many sources of enteric pathogens, including raw meat, and stocks of bacteria held in academic research laboratories under low security. Of all potential biological weapons, the enteric bacteria are probably the easiest to grow and handle. Fortunately, these pathogens rarely cause death in healthy individuals. As such, they could mainly be used to incapacitate people. The main risk from these pathogens is large-scale distribution through food or water. Most infections with enteric bacteria can be treated with antibiotics, and with some exceptions, they are susceptible to environmental degradation and inactivation by disinfectant chemicals.

12.4 Viruses of Concern

Smallpox

Smallpox virus is also known as variola virus. It is a relatively large virus that is a member of the family Poxviridae. It is surrounded by a fatty envelope and uses DNA as its genetic material. Smallpox virus is related to cowpox and monkeypox. Poxviruses are unique because unlike most viruses, they encode their own unique molecular machinery needed for viral replication in host cells.

Smallpox disease begins with an incubation period of around twelve days, during which the virus infects various cells, normally beginning in the lungs. After this period, the number of viruses in the body increases rapidly, and ulcers begin to form on the skin. Ulcers appear first in the mouth and then on the skin of the arms and hands. Afterwards, the ulcers spread throughout the entire body and sometimes appear on the eyes. Victims are most contagious during the time that ulcers are forming on the skin. In a small percentage of cases, smallpox victims develop no visible blisters. Rather, they hemorrhage throughout the body, resulting in extensive internal bleeding and a high fatality rate.

Smallpox is a unique biological weapon because it is extremely contagious and it kills a significant percentage of the people it infects. But most importantly, it is unique because no natural cases have occurred since disease was eradicated. Since it was declared eradicated in 1979, the only remaining stocks of smallpox virus have been supposedly confined to two locations, The Centers for Disease Control and Prevention in the United States and the Institute of Virus Preparations in Russia. Unfortunately, security in Russia has been lax since the fall of the Soviet Union and there is a chance that terrorists or rogue governments have acquired stocks of the virus. In the past, people were vaccinated against smallpox, which greatly reduced the potential for pandemic spread. Since the virus was eradicated, however, only certain members of the military have been vaccinated. Thus, if a virulent strain of smallpox were to be accidentally released from a laboratory or used as a biological weapon, it could feasibly kill a full third of the human population within a few months. As a result, some countries, including the United States, have begun to stockpile smallpox vaccine in case of an outbreak. Although no treatment exists for smallpox once infection has begun and the virus can persist on contaminated objects for extended periods of time, it is sensitive to most chemical disinfectants.

Equine encephalitis viruses

Equine encephalitis viruses are members of the virus family Togaviridae. These viruses use RNA as genetic material and are surrounded by a thin, fatty coating. They can infect horses, but the predominant mode of transmission in nature is from infected rodents or birds to humans through mosquitoes. Many strains of equine encephalitis virus cause disease in nature. In the United States, Eastern equine encephalitis virus is most common, but Western and Venezuelan equine encephalitis are also a concern.

Equine encephalitis disease is characterized by an incubation period of a few days to one week followed by fever, chills, headache, weakness, and general discomfort. Approximately 2 to 4 percent of those infected develop encephalitis, or swelling of the brain. Disease usually lasts from one to two weeks and the overall mortality rate is approximately 1 percent. No vaccines are known to prevent equine encephalitis virus infection and no treatments are known for the disease.

Equine encephalitis viruses have the potential to be used as biological weapons because they are relatively stable in the environment and can be transmitted by the aerosol route. Since equine encephalitis viruses produce incapacitating infections that kill about one in one hundred people, a deliberate dissemination of the virus could infect thousands of people and cause great psychological distress among the uninfected. Person to person spread has not been demonstrated, so the potential for a pandemic as a result of use as a biological weapon is low.

Hemorrhagic viruses

Hemorrhagic viruses are those that cause internal bleeding during the normal course of infection. Hemorrhagic viruses include hantavirus, Dengue virus, Lassa virus, Marburg virus, and Ebola virus. Marburg virus and Ebola virus are the two most deadly hemorrhagic viruses. They are both members of the family Filoviridae, meaning that they are elongated in shape and use RNA as genetic material. During infection, hemorrhagic viruses replicate rapidly. In nature, hemorrhagic virus outbreaks are limited to small geographical regions. These regions are defined by the ecosystems that support the animal and insect vectors of the disease. Hantavirus outbreaks are confined to the southwestern United States and are spread by dry rodent feces. Lassa, Marburg, and Ebola virus outbreaks are normally confined to West and Central Africa, where people come into contact with contaminated monkeys. Dengue fever outbreaks are observed in tropical equatorial regions where a particular species of mosquito spreads the disease.

Hemorrhagic viral infections are characterized by incubation periods of one to a few days followed by high fever, bleeding of soft tissues including the gums, and high fatality rates. Hemorrhagic viruses are extremely deadly. For example, Ebola virus has killed up to 90 percent of those infected in some outbreaks, and usually kills at least 30 percent of the people it infects. No treatment currently exists for infections with hemorrhagic viruses. Vaccine development is difficult because the viruses are risky to handle and study and vaccines are not likely to be profitable.

Hemorrhagic viruses (especially Ebola and Marburg virus) are some of the most frightening potential biological weapons. They quickly kill large percentages of the people they infect and infections can spread rapidly. In addition, very little is known about them because they can only be handled safely in a few laboratories scattered around the world. The majority of infections from Marburg and Ebola viruses appear to have come from contact with blood from infected monkeys and humans, but transmission of the virus through air remains a disturbing possibility. If Marburg or Ebola virus were to be disseminated deliberately through aerosols or other means, the ensuing outbreak of disease could be catastrophic.

Norovirus

Norovirus is a very small, round virus that belongs to the family Caliciviridae. Noroviruses infect the gastrointestinal tract and produce profuse diarrhea and vomiting. Infected people shed billions of viruses in their feces. In nature, noroviruses are transmitted through contaminated food and water. Although the infective dose is still under investigation, one or a few noroviruses are though to be all that is needed to initiate an infection.

Norovirus disease consists of a very short incubation period, from eight hours to about three days. After incubation, victims experience diarrhea and forceful vomiting. Many viruses are excreted by infected people during this time and can be detected in vomit and feces. For this reason, outbreaks of norovirus can be explosive in crowded places like cruise ships and classrooms. No treatment currently exists for norovirus infection and people are not known to develop protective immunity after infection.

Infections are very rarely fatal, but are almost always incapacitating. If used as biological weapons, noroviruses could be distributed through water or food. However, noroviruses cannot currently be grown and concentrated in the laboratory. Because noroviruses are protected by a sturdy protein shell and contain no internal liquid, they are persistent in the environment.

Hepatitis A virus

Hepatitis A virus is a small, round virus that is a member of the family Picornaviridae. After ingestion, the virus infects liver cells, where it multiplies rapidly and causes temporary damage to the liver. During infection, the virus is shed in feces in great numbers. Because hepatitis A viruses are protected by a sturdy protein shell and contain no internal liquid, they are persistent in the environment.

Hepatitis A disease begins with an incubation period of between fifteen and forty-five days. After incubation, the virus multiplies rapidly, damaging liver cells and reducing liver function. The characteristic sign of hepatitis is jaundice, or yellowing of the skin, and symptoms of infection usually last for around two weeks. Infections are fatal in approximately one in 100 cases. Lifelong immunity is usually developed after infection with hepatitis A virus. Treatment of hepatitis A is not normally necessary and a vaccine is available that can prevent infections.

Although hepatitis A virus is not a classical biological weapon, it may be highly attractive to terrorist groups. First, the virus can be obtained easily from people with natural infections, which are especially common in developing countries. Hepatitis virus can also be grown in many microbiology laboratories, which means that viral stocks could be created with relative ease. Because the virus is resistant to degradation in the environment and is highly infectious, it is a candidate for deliberate transmission through water.

12.5 Toxins as Biological Weapons

Biological toxins are large molecules produced by living organisms that damage cells in the human body. A number of microorganisms produce toxins during growth. Many characteristic aspects of diseases are caused entirely by the action of toxins on the body. For example, diarrhea during cholera infection is caused by the production of potent cholera A-B toxin in the intestines. Cholera A-B toxin causes intestinal cells to actively excrete salts, which effectively reverses the normal digestion process and results in severe diarrhea and loss of water. Other toxins act on more critical sites within the body, like neurons and red blood cells, interfering with the body's ability to transmit nerve impulses and oxygen. Some neuronal toxins from bacteria are so potent that less than an ounce of pure toxin could kill the entire human population.

Biological toxins have the potential to be used as biological weapons. First, they can be produced and concentrated in the laboratory with only moderate skill and investment. Second, many toxins resist degradation in the environment and inactivation by chemicals. Lastly, they are so potent that even small amounts delivered through food, air or water could lead to numerous deaths. Their potency also makes them difficult to detect in the environment, even at dangerous levels. The two toxins in particular with high potential impact if used as biological weapons are Staphylococcal enterotoxin B and botulinum toxin. Staphlococcal enterotoxin B is a non-lethal toxin produced by the bacterium *Staphylococcus aureus* that has the potential to be spread as a weapon because it can withstand high temperatures and can be disseminated through food, water or air. When ingested, the toxin causes classical symptoms of food poisoning, but when inhaled it can causes severe systemic illness including fever that lasts for up to two weeks. In high doses, Staphylococcal enterotoxin B also causes shortness of breath, organ failure, and death. Botulinum toxin is another toxin of concern, produced by the anaerobic bacterium *Clostridium botulinum.* Exposure to this toxin results in botulism. Botulism is a flaccid paralysis of the body caused when botulinum toxin binds to the ends of neurons and prevents the release of the neurotransmitter acetylcholine, thereby preventing transmission of nerve impulses. If the toxin dose is high enough, the nerve impulses responsible for breathing and heart function become blocked, leading to death. Botulism can be treated by artificial respiration until the body recovers, but such services would not likely be available in the event that the toxin were to be used as a biological weapon. Botulinum toxin is the most potent toxin known to man. In fact, just one milligram of this toxin is enough to kill one million guinea pigs. The potency, versatility, and availability of biological toxins make them major concerns as biological weapons.

12.6 Chapter Summary

Humans have a long history of using microorganisms as weapons. In the age of modern science, many harmful microorganisms can be grown and cultivated in the laboratory with relative ease, potentially putting the power of these weapons into the hands of terrorists and rogue governments. Biological weapons have been used at least twice in the United States already. In one case *Salmonella* was used to influence a local election, and in another case, deadly *Bacillus anthracis* was used to target senators and the media, killing five people. The United States Centers for Disease Control and Prevention separates potential biological weapons into three categories depending on their potential to cause harm. Category A agents include hemorrhagic viruses, smallpox, the bacterium that causes anthrax, and other highly transmissible or virulent microorganisms. Microbial toxins are also included in Category A, because they can be stable in the environment and are extremely potent. Category B agents include pathogens with moderate virulence but high accessibility or transmission for spread, like enteric bacterial pathogens and viruses that are not spread by aerosols. Category C agents have less potential to be used as weapons, like the bacterium that causes tuberculosis.

Chapter 13

Microbial Risk Assessment

13.1 Chapter Preview

Microbiologists use a well-defined, validated method called quantitative risk assessment to determine the probability that contact with a microorganism will result in infection. Microbial risk assessment consists of four distinct steps. First, the hazard is identified. Then, an appropriate dose-response model is chosen from scientific literature to assess the likely outcome of the exposure. Next, an individual's level of exposure to the hazard is quantified. Finally, the risk of infection is characterized in terms of its magnitude and related to risks posed by other hazards. Risks assessed in this fashion are extremely valuable because they are based on science and have been repeatedly validated by retrospective analyses of attack rates during outbreaks of disease. Risk assessment techniques are valuable to lawyers and judges because they can be used to assess the probability that a microorganism has caused or will cause a disease in a given circumstance based on scientific theory, rather than subjective intuition.

13.2 Introduction

People in the United States have a generally high awareness that microorganisms pose risks, but rarely judge the magnitude of microbial risks accurately. Risks of infection are implicitly communicated to people in many ways, including through insidious advertisements touting consumer products that "Kill Germs" or are "Antibacterial." Quantitative risk assessments help put risks into perspective for non-experts in a reliable, scientific way.

Consider a real example of a situation in which quantitative microbial risk assessment was useful. In the 1990s, citizens in the United States and abroad began to voice concerns about the potential risks of infection from recycling pathogen-loaded human sewage sludge by spreading it on farmland as fertilizer. Although farmers had been land-applying sewage sludge for decades, the issue came to light in the 1990s because homes were being constructed in increasingly rural areas to accommodate an expanding suburban America. The result was that some neighborhoods found themselves positioned immediately downwind of rural sewage sludge land application sites. In many areas, great numbers of people were subjected to strong odors for long periods of time. It was obvious to those affected that gasses from the land application site were making their way through air to communities. Many citizens feared that pathogens from the sewage sludge were being transported through air as well. By 2000, some citizens' infection concerns bordered on hysteria. Anti-sludge literature circulated in academia and on the Internet, describing cases of disease from sludge and warning people that they were at risk of infection. Industry literature was also circulated, suggesting that there was no risk to health. In the meantime, numerous lawsuits were filed and industrial sludge-appliers settled lawsuits out of court. Some counties in Florida, California, and Pennsylvania banned land application of sewage sludge altogether citing public health concerns. In 2002, The National Science Foundation Water Quality Center at the University of Arizona received funding to conduct a quantified microbial risk assessment to address the size of the problem. First, aerosolized fecal pathogens were identified as the hazard. Then, exposure intensity was assessed using over 500 air samples taken at land-application sites throughout the country. Then, exposure durations were estimated for people in communities. Based on well-studied relationships between pathogen dose and infection probability, daily and annual risks of infection were calculated. As it turned out, risks of infection were extremely low to nearby communities and risks were low but manageable to the workers who applied the sludge. In 2004, the data and risk calculations were peer-reviewed, published, and circulated throughout industry, academia, and government. The quantitative risk assessment effectively communicated actual risks of infection to stakeholders in the problem. By 2006, fears were largely assuaged in communities and industrial sludge-appliers were well-informed of the potential risks to workers.

13.3 Risk Perception

Many factors contribute to people's perception of risks, and that determines how people react to risks of infection from microorganisms. In general, risks are perceived to be greater when they are difficult to understand, unexpected, catastrophic, involuntary, their impact is delayed, or children primarily are affected. Risks are perceived to be lower when they are understandable, controllable, voluntary, and clear benefits are associated with the risky activity (Covello 1988).

People sometimes grossly misjudge the risks associated with infectious diseases because microorganisms are difficult to see and understand and they have delayed or uncertain effects. For example, if a group of scientists in lab coats were to enter a theater containing 100 people with a loudspeaker and inform the audience that, "Instruments have detected two anthrax bacteria spores currently airborne in this room," panic would likely ensue and people would probably assume that only ninety-eight of the original 100 people would survive the event. But panic is not necessary in this hypothetical case. The risk to individuals in the theater is actually very, very low. All together, the theater occupants breathe less than 100 cubic meters of air in an hour. If the theater is of normal size, then it probably has a volume of more than 1,000 square meters. If everyone left the theater within the hour, then the likelihood of any one person inhaling a single spore is only ten percent. Then there is the dose-response relationship of Anthrax to consider. According to most accounts, at least 1,000 anthrax spores must be inhaled to produce disease in an average person. Thus, a quick consideration of the actual level of exposure and the established dose-response relationship means that the likelihood of death from one or two inhaled anthrax spores is very low. In this case, infection would be a remote possibility, but the perception of risk would be extremely high nonetheless.

Understanding microbial risk perception is fundamental to handling infectious disease cases appropriately. Thus, lawyers and judges may wish to consider the layperson's perception of the infectious disease at hand: Is it understood by the layperson, like the common cold, or is it unfamiliar, like anthrax and toxic mold? Does it primarily affect children? Does it result in death? Are the effects delayed? Can the infection be controlled? Knowing the answers to these questions can help lawyers and judges communicate risks and infections accurately and objectively to others.

13.4 Usefulness of Microbial Risk Assessment

Quantitative microbial risk assessments are important because they replace risk perception with risk calculation based on science. To perform a quantified microbial risk assessment, one must identify many different routes of exposure to a hazard and carefully measure the contribution of each. One must also understand the strengths and weaknesses of past scientific studies, which describe the relationship between pathogen dose and host response. Empirically determined exposures to pathogens must then be objectively linked to the dose-response models. Finally, one must have the confidence to accept the risk predicted by the scientific model and apply that to relevant decisions with respect to public health. By doing so, the scientist combines many fields of study to produce one very useful estimation.

Microbial risk assessments are crucial to modern policy decision-making. For example, the United States Environmental Protection Agency (USEPA) has set the acceptable risk of infection from drinking water at one in ten thousand per year. Since the acceptable risk of infection has been determined, the USEPA can back-calculate what the maximum exposure to a given microorganism must be to achieve risks of infection lower than one in ten thousand.

Another reason that quantified risk assessments are valuable is that a great deal of exposure data must be empirically measured before the risk assessments will be scientifically acceptable, which helps put exposure into perspective. For example, someone living in a home contaminated with toxic mold may feel like they're breathing in spores with every breath, but scientific investigation would indicate that the real exposure level is probably closer to one spore per every thousand breaths, if that, because toxic mold is normally damp to the touch and difficult to aerosolize. Furthermore, relevant calculations for risk assessments are normally presented along with exposure data and predicted risks. This provides an open and transparent forum for discussion of the importance of several predictors of disease outcome such as intensity of exposure, exposure duration, virulence of the microorganism, age and occupation.

13.5 The Process of Microbial Risk Assessment

A. Hazard identification

The first step in a quantitative microbial risk assessment is to identify all microbial hazards, then focus the rest of the risk assessment on the relevant hazards. Microbial hazards are normally identified by analysis of clinical or environmental samples. For example, if one were to investigate the risk of bacterial infection as a result of eating food prepared in a hospital, one would analyze representative food samples for the presence of several pathogens. If various strains of *Salmonella* were discovered, then the risk assessment could focus on the risk posed by that particular type of bacterium.

B. Dose-response modeling

As Figure 13.1 shows, an appropriate dose-response model is chosen from the scientific literature. Over the years, microbiologists have amassed an impressive body of information related to the relationship between microbial exposure and disease outcome. Much of this information comes from volunteer human inoculation and feeding studies, where people are exposed to various doses of pathogens and the rate of infection and disease is measured. Information about more virulent pathogens usually comes from animal inoculation studies. Information is available for many pathogens via various routes of infection, such as inhalation, dermal contact, and ingestion. After information is gathered, it is fitted to an appropriate mathematical model. For viruses, it has been shown that an exponential model known as the one-hit exponential model is highly representative of the dose-response relationship. This model assumes that a single intact viral particle is capable of initiating infection, and that the probability of developing disease increases exponentially with the dose. The dose-response relationship can be modeled by the beta-poisson equation for many bacteria, including *Salmonella*. This equation is very similar to that used for viruses at low doses, but predicts that the number of infected individuals increases less rapidly at high doses.

C. Exposure assessment

The level of exposure to a microorganism is a crucial variable in risk assessment and can have a major impact on the final calculated risk of infection or disease. Exposure data must be gathered for the appropriate exposure route. For example, if one were to base an assessment of the risk posed by drinking water only on exposure to microorganisms during dermal contact, a major source of exposure would not enter into the final risk calculation. Exposure data must also be handled skillfully from a statistical perspective. Microbiological data is frequently more variable in nature than data encountered in other fields. For this reason, an experienced microbiologist or statistician should analyze exposure data to assure that the most accurate estimates of exposure are fed into the dose-response equations.

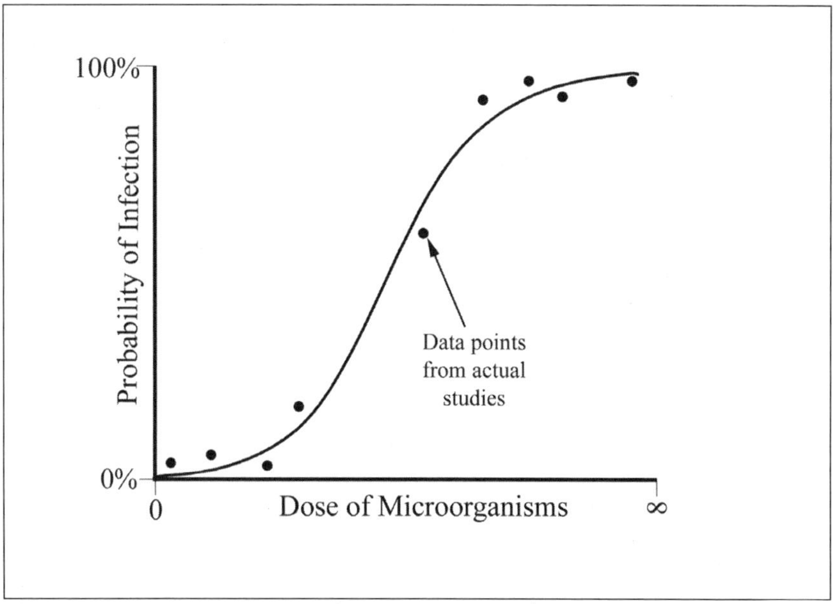

Figure 13.1 *A representative dose response curve.*

D. Risk characterization

Risk characterization estimates the impact of an exposure to a microorganism. Usually, impact is expressed in terms of the risk of infection or disease. Risks of infection or disease are calculated by plugging the expected range of exposure into the appropriate dose-response model. If the exposure information is in terms of germs encountered per hour, then the risk will be "risk of infection per hour of exposure." If longer-term risk calculations are desired, it is appropriate to calculate daily infection risks and then calculate lifetime risks from those values, as probabilities. This method can also be used to estimate risks of infections to populations as long as risks are treated mathematically as probabilities.

13.6 Reliability of Microbial Risk Assessments

Predictions made by microbial risk assessments can be validated using past information on outbreaks of disease where exposures were known. For example, microbiologists used the massive waterborne Cryptosporidium outbreak that occurred in Milwaukee in 1994 to see how well risk assessment models would have predicted the outcome. This outbreak showed that predicted rates of disease were within 25 percent of actual rates of disease. The book Quantitative Microbial Risk Assessment, by Haas, et al. (1999), provides a thorough analysis of risk assessment process and examples of risk model validation. In addition, the book provides many dose-response models useful for calculating microbial risks.

13.7 Chapter Summary

The public is aware that microbes pose infection risks, but the magnitudes of these risks are often misjudged. Infection risks may be perceived to be great because infections are involuntary, hard to understand, their effects are delayed, and they can be catastrophic. Quantitative microbial risk assessments are an effective way to calculate and communicate infection risks based on science. They are performed in four steps. First, microbial hazards are identified through investigation. The risk assessment then focuses only on microorganisms that are suspected to be a hazard for the exposure scenario in question. Second, an appropriate dose-response model is chosen or created from the scientific literature. Third, the degree of exposure is calculated to approximate the likelihood that a person will come into contact (and therefore have the potential to be infected by) a microorganism. Last, the amount of exposure is entered into the dose-response model, yielding the potential impact of exposure. Quantitative microbial risk assessments are useful in many ways. Importantly, their predictions can be checked from time to time by comparing them to what is observed in actual infectious disease outbreaks.

References

Brands, D., Inman, A., Gerba, C., Mare, C., Billington, S., Saif, L., Levine, J., and Joens, L. "Prevalence of Salmonella spp. in Oysters in the United States." *Applied and Environmental Microbiology*. 71:893-897 (2005).

Brooks, J., Tanner, B., Gerba, C., Haas, C., and Pepper, I. "Estimation of bioaerosol risk of infection to residents adjacent to a land applied biosolids site using an empirically derived transport model." *Journal of Applied Microbiology*. 98: 397-405 (2005).

Buckman, R. *Human Wildlife*. Baltimore: The Johns Hopkins University Press (2002).

Carducci, A., Tozzi, E., Rubulotta, E., Casini, B., Cantiani, L., Rovini, E., Muscillo, M., and Pacini. R. "Assessing airborne biological hazard from urban wastewater treatment." *Water Research*. 34:1173-1178 (2000).

Clark, C., Ragnar, R., and Larsson, L. "Levels of Gram-negative Bacteria, Aspergillus Fumigatus, Dust, and Endotoxin at Compost Plants." *Applied and Environmental Microbiology*. 45:1501-1505 (1983).

Covello, V., von Winterfieldt, D., and Slovic, P. "Risk Communication: A Review of the Literature." *Risk Analysis*. 3: 171-182 (1988).

Craun, G., and Calderon, R. In: *Manual of Water Supply Practices, 1st Edition*. Denver: American Water Works Association Publishing (1999).

Craun, G., and Calderon, R., and Craun, M. "Outbreaks Associated with Recreational Water in the United States." *International Journal of Health Research* 15:243-62 (2005).

D'Hondt, S., Rutherford, S., and Spivack, A. "Metabolic Activity of Subsurface Life in Deep-sea Sediments." *Science*. 295:2067-2070 (2002).

Diamond, J. *Guns, Germs, and Steel, The Fates of Human Societies*. New York: W. W. Norton and Company, Inc. (1999).

DuPont, H., Chappel, C., Sterling, C., Okhuysen, P., Rose, J., and W. Jakubowski. "The Infectivity of Cryposporidium Paruum in Healthy Volunteers." *New England Journal of Medicine* 332: 855-859 (1995).

Dye, C., Scheele, S., Dolin, P., Pathania, V., and Raviglione, M. "Consensus Statement. Global Burden of Tuberculosis: Estimated Incidence, Prevalence, and Mortality by Country." *Journal of the American Medical Association.* 18:677-686 (1999).

Epstein, P. "Algal Blooms in the Spread and Persistence of Cholera." *Biosystems.* 31:209-221 (1993).

Filetoth, Z. *Hospital-Acquired Infection.* Pennsylvania: Whurr Publishers (2003).

Friis, R., and Sellers, T. *Epidemiology for Public Health Practice, Second Edition.* Maryland: Aspen Publishers (1999).

Fujioka, R., and Narikawa, O. "Effect of Sunlight on Enumeration of Indicator Bacteria under Field Conditions. *Applied and Environmental Microbiology.* 44: 395-401 (1982).

Gerba, C., and Bitton, G. *Groundwater Pollution Microbiology.* New York: John Wiley and Sons (1984).

Gerba, C., and Kayed, D. "Caliciviruses: a major cause of foodborne illness." *Journal of Food Science.* 68:1136-1142 (2003).

Gleeson, C., and Gray, N. *The Coliform Index and Waterborne Disease.* London: E. and F.N. Spon (1997).

Graves, N., "Economics and prevention of hospital-acquired infection." *Emerging Infectious Diseases.* 10:561-566 (2004).

Haas, C., Rose, J., and Gerba, C. "Framework for microbial dose-response relationships." *Quantitative Microbial Risk Assessment.* New York: John Wiley and Sons (1999).

Herz, J., and Taylor, K. *Toxic Mold Litigation.* Tucson: Lawyers and Judges Publishing Company (2005).

Hibler, C., and Hancock, C. *Waterborne Giardiasis. Drinking Water Microbiology.* New York: Springer-Verlag (1990).

Hossain, M., Ahmed, M., and Ghannoum, M. "Attributes of Stachybotrys chartarum and its association with human disease." *Journal of Allergy and Clinical Immunology.* 113:200-208 (2004).

Hoxie, N., Davis, J., and Vergeront, J. "Cryptosporidiosis-associated mortality following a massive waterborne outbreak in Milwaukee, Wisconsin." Madison, Wisconsin: Report of Wisconsin Department of Health and Social Services (1996).

Jarvis, W. "Outbreaks associated with healthcare delivery." In: *Disinfection, Sterilization and Antisepsis*, Ed. Rutala, W. Washington, D.C.: Association for Professionals in Infection Control and Epidemiology, Inc. (2003).

Jay, James M. *Modern Food Microbiology, Sixth Edition*. Maryland: Aspen Publishers (2000).

Keeffe, E. "Occupational risk for Hepatitis A: A literature-based analysis." *Journal of Clinical Gastroenterology.* 38:440-448 (2004).

Kilvington, S., and Price, J. "Survival of Legionella pneumophila within cysts of Acanthamoeba polyphaga following chlorine exposure." *Journal of Applied Bacteriology* 68:519-525 (1990).

Kruse, H., and Sorum, H. "Transfer of multiple drug resistance plasmids between bacteria of diverse origins in natural microenvironments." *Applied and Environmental Microbiology*. 60:4015-4021 (1994).

Larson, E., Gomez-duarte, C., Lee, L., Della-Latta, P., Kain, D., and Keswick, B. "Microbial flora of hands of homemakers." *American Journal of Infection Control*. 31:72-79 (2003).

LeChevallier, M. "The case for maintaining a disinfectant residual." *The Journal of the American Water Works Association.* 91:86-94 (2003).

LeChevallier, M., Gullick, R., Karim, M., Friedman, M, and Funk, J. "The potential for health risks from intrusion of contaminants into the distribution system from pressure transients." *Journal of Water and Health.* 1:3-14 (2003).

Lindsay, J., "Chronic Sequelae of Foodborne Disease." *Emerging Infectious Diseases*. 3:443-452 (1997).

MacKenzie, W., Hoxie, N., Proctor, M., Gradus, M., Blair, K., Peterson, D. Kazmierczak, J., Addiss, D., Fox, K., and Rose, J. "A massive outbreak in Milwaukee of Cryposporidium infection transmitted through the public water supply." *New England Journal of Medicine*. 331:161-167 (1994).

Madigan, T., Martinko, J., and J. Parker. *Brock Biology of Microorganisms, (9th ed).*"Upper Saddle River: Prentice Hall (2000).

Maier, R., Pepper, I., and C. Gerba. *Environmental Microbiology, (1st ed).* London: Academic Press (2000).

Marciano-Cabral, F., MacLean, R., Mensah, A., and LaPat-Polasko, L. "Identification of Naegleria fowleri in domestic water sources by nested PCR." *Applied and Environmental Microbiology.* 69: 5864-5869 (2003).

Marler, W. D. "How to keep your focus on food safety." *Food Safety Magazine.* 11:64-68 (2005).

Martone, W., Jarvis, W., Culver, D., and Haley, R. "Incidence and nature of endemic and epidemic nosocomial infections." In: Bennet, J., Brachman, P., eds. *Hospital Infections (3rd ed.).* Boston: Little, Brown (1992).

Mauchline, W., James, B., Fitzgeorge, R., Dennis, P., and Keevil, C. "Growth temperature reversibly modulates the virulence of Legionella pneumophila." *Infection and Immunity* 62:2995-2997 (1994).

Moberg, L. "Good manufacturing practices for refrigerated foods." *Journal of Food Protection.* 52:363-367 (1989).

Parham, P. *The Immune System, (1st ed).* New York: Garland Science Publishing (2000).

Paul, E., and Clark, F. *Soil Microbiology and Biochemistry.* San Diego: Academic Press (1989).

Payment, P., and Franco, E. "Clostriduim perfringens and somatic coliphages as indicators of the efficiency of drinking water treatment for viruses and protozoan cysts." *Applied and Environmental Microbiology.* 59: 2418-2424 (1993).

Pepper, I. "Plasmid Profiles. Methods of Soil Analysis." *Part 2: Microbiological and Biochemical Properties.* Madison: Soil Science Society of America (1994).

Rajan, S., and Saiman, L. "Pulmonary infections in patients with cystic fibrosis." *Seminars in Respiratory Infection.* 17:47-56 (2002).

Rivera, S., Hazen, T., and Toranzos, G. "Isolation of fecal coliforms from pristine sites in a tropical rain forest." *Applied and Environmental Microbiology.* 54: 513-517 (1988).

Rubin, K. "What water suppliers need to know about toxic tort litigation." *Drinking Water Regulation and Health.* F. Pontius, Ed. New York: John Wiley and Sons (2003).

Russell, A. "Link between germicide use and antibiotic resistance." In: *Disinfection, Sterilization and Antisepsis,* Ed. Rutala, W. Washington, D.C.: Association for Professionals in Infection Control and Epidemiology, Inc. (2003).

Short, L., and Bell, D. "Risk of occupational infection with blood-borne pathogens in operating and delivery room settings." *American Journal of Infection Control.* 21:343-350 (1993).

Simonsen, B., Bryan, F., and Christian, J. "Prevention and control of foodborne salmonellosis through application of Hazard Analysis Critical Control Point (HACCP)." *International Journal of Food Microbiology.* 4:227-247 (1987).

Sperber, W.H. "The modern HACCP system." *Food Technology.* 46:116-120 (1991).

Stine, S., Pepper, I., and Gerba, C. "Contribution of drinking water to the weekly intake of heterotrophic bacteria from diet in the United States." *Water Research* 39:2337-263 (2005).

Stine, S., Song, I., Choi, C., and Gerba, C. "Application of microbial risk assessment to the development of standards for enteric pathogens in water used to irrigate fresh produce." *Journal of Food Protection.* 68:913-918 (2005).

Tanner, B., and Gerba, C., "Application of the Ct concept for determining the disinfection of microorganisms in water." *Journal of the Swimming Pool and Spa Industry.* 5:8-14 (2004).

Tanner, B., and Gerba, C. "Outbreaks of Legionella associated with hot tubs and spas." *Journal of the Swimming Pool and Spa Industry.* In press (2006).

Tanner, B., and Gerba, C. "Update on outbreaks of Cryptosporidium associated with swimming pools." *Journal of the Swimming Pool and Spa Industry.* 5: 1-10 (2005).

Tanner, B., Brooks, J., Josephson, K, Haas, C., Gerba, C., and Pepper, I. "Occupational risk of infection from biosolids applied to land." *Applied and Environmental Microbiology* (Submitted, 2006).

Tanner, B., Kuwahara, S., Gerba, C., and Reynolds, K. "Evaluation of electrochemically generated ozone for the disinfection of water and wastewater." *Water Science and Technology*. 50:19-25 (2004).

United Nations AIDS, AIDS Epidemic Update, 2003. Retrieved from the World Wide Web, 05/2004. http://www.unaids.org/Unaids/EN/Resources/Publications (2004).

United States Department of Agriculture Economic Research Service. Internet. http://www.ers.usda.gov/briefing/FoodborneDisease/Features.htm (2004).

White, D., and Fenner, F. *Medical Virology (4th ed)*. San Diego: Academic Press (1994).

Yu, D., and Thompson, G. "Clinical, epidemiological and pathogenic aspects of reactive arthritis." *Food Microbiology*. 11:97-108 (1994).

About the Author

Benjamin Tanner, Ph.D. received a Doctor of Philosophy degree in Microbiology and Immunology from the University of Arizona in 2005, where renowned microbiologist Dr. Charles Gerba served as his advisor. He has published a number of articles in peer-reviewed scholarly journals and presented his research to various audiences in academia, industry, and government. In addition, he has done collaborative research with the United States Environmental Protection Agency, United States Department of Agriculture, and the National Science Foundation Water Quality Center at the University of Arizona.

Dr. Tanner has focused his academic and professional endeavors on preventing environmentally mediated disease transmission. Some of his major achievements include helping to define the impact of water quality on the action of disinfectants, evaluating environmental specimens for microorganisms in support of litigation, assessing risks of infection from aerosols generated during the reuse of municipal waste, and assisting with the identification of noroviruses as the cause of gastrointestinal disease outbreaks on cruise ships. Dr. Tanner currently works as a microbiologist for the Clorox Company, where he develops disinfectants that help prevent disease transmission.

Index

Forensic Aspects of Communication Sciences and Disorders #6311

Dennis C. Tanner

Communication science and disorders play an important part in many legal cases, particularly accident, disability, and medical malpractice litigation. It is often necessary to determine the nature and extent of injuries and the effects they have on the ability to communicate and, therefore, on the quality of life. Dr. Tanner's book provides a comprehensive overview of human communication and the myriad of diseases, disorders, deficiencies, and defects that can lay waste to it.

When litigating these cases, lawyers and judges are often thrown into a new and complex world of language disorders in children: aphasia, apraxia of speech, disorientation, phonological deficits, verbal paraphasias, dysphagia, silent aspiration, stuttering, and so on.

This book emphasizes those issues important in litigation. It will serve as a worthwhile reference, cutting through the technical terminology and allowing an understanding of the relevant scientific and professional issues associated with human communication and its disorders.

Topics include:

- A profile of communication sciences and disorders
- Dysphagia (a swallowing disorder in both children and adults)
- Neurogenic communication disorders
- Communication disorders resulting from head and neck injuries
- Voice and resonance disorders
- Childhood communication disorders
- Communication and dementia
- Deafness, hearing loss, and audiological assessment